40 Years, 40 Lessons

40 Years,
40 Lessons

40 Years, 40 Lessons

Mastering Asset Management & Reliability

Gary Tyne

40 Years, 40 Lessons
Gary Tyne
ISBN: 978 1 7391878-9-7

Publisher: Ousha Demello, The Uplifted Publishing
Cover & Book Interior Designed by The Uplifted Publishing
Edited by The Uplifted Publishing

Foreword

Gary Tyne offers lots of practical lessons in this easy-to-read and practical set of stories and experiences that he has accumulated over the past forty years.

I've known Gary for many years now, beginning with our work together at a chemical plant in England. It was an enlightening and entertaining experience for both of us as we walked about the plant, met with various staff, and generally worked together to assess their current practices and establish a sustainable improvement plan. He will enlighten you on that particular experience, along with so many others.

You should take away many lessons, some simple and others more profound, as you read his book. Properly applied, you will be able to use these learnings simply and practically in your plant for substantial improvement.

My best wishes for your success in doing so.

Ron Moore
Managing Partner
The RM Group, Inc.
Knoxville, TN 37934

Acknowledgement

A massive thank you and a few well-deserved shout-outs go to...

My Wife, Sharon, for your unwavering love, patience, and support throughout this journey. You've stood by me through every mile, every challenge, and every chapter of this story. I couldn't have done it without you.

My Son Connor, for making me the happiest man on the planet... Thank you for being understanding when Dad wasn't always home. You're my greatest adventure.

My Dad, for your love and support and for pointing me in the right career direction when I was 16, that one piece of advice shaped everything that followed. Thank you.

My Mum (RIP), I miss you every day. Thank you for telling me, 'Get to Australia, there's nothing around here', I did listen. And you were right.

My Sister Jo, for her love and for constantly telling me I can do it. You believed in me even when I didn't believe in myself. Your faith in me helped carry me through.

Acknowledgement

My Friends, across the globe, thank you for putting up with my endless travel stories, again and again. Your patience, humour, and friendship have meant the world.

To all my former Work Colleagues in every company I've worked, thank you for the shared lessons, laughs, and learning. You helped shape the professional I've become.

To my customers, thank you for trusting me, challenging me, and teaching me in return. You've been some of my greatest mentors.

A few special mentions, for your influence, friendship, and inspiration over the years from the beginning of my journey to present day: Andrew Fraser, Andrew Wilkinson (RIP), Andy Lonsdale, Andy Gailey and Jenny Ambler, Bill Keeter, Chris Cassidy, Dave Elson, Dean Gano, Gary Smith, Gilbert Hamambi, Ian Anderton, Ian Price, Jason Apps, Jason Ballentine, Jo Wright, Joe Beckett, John Griffiths, John McEntyre, Kieran Sager, Mariana Batalim, Mark Crosbie, Mark Gurney, Mark Michael, Martin Hincks, Martin Thomas, Martin Williamson, Melissa Cameron, Mick Drew, Mike Gibbons, Miles Fox (RIP), Neville Jones, Ozan Catikli, Pete McCoombe, PJ Cloete, Rachel Evans, Rachael Cowin, Rodney Bury, Ron Moore, Steve Collinson, Steve Maskell, Steve Vardy, Steve Flanagan, Steve Stehr, Stu Bevan, Tony Gales, Tommy Nair, Wes Gano, Zhelyazko Kodzhabashev.
Thank you for walking parts of this journey with me.

Acknowledgement

To Mobius Connect Conversations (mobiusconnect.com) – Thank you for inviting me onto your podcast platform and giving me a space to share my voice and stories.

To Mainstream Conferences (www.mainstreamcommunity.com) – Thank you for allowing me to launch this book via their first UK Conference. What a moment to remember.

And finally, I would like to sincerely thank my publisher, Ousha Demello, for your wonderful support and encouragement. This book would not have been possible without your commitment to bringing these stories and lessons to life.

"Your life is the sum of your experiences.
When you look back on your life, the richness of those experiences will determine how full a life you've led."
Bill Perkins.

"Reliability isn't something you achieve once.

It's something you build every day."

Table of Contents

Table of Contents

Introduction

INTRODUCTION

"Reliability is not about fixing failures.
It's about not having them."
Ron Moore

When I first stepped into the world of maintenance and reliability over 40 years ago, I didn't have a roadmap. What I did have was a brand-new toolbox, a few mentors, a willingness to learn, and a stubborn determination to figure things out. Back then, we diagnosed machines by ear, I mean listening really carefully, tracking spares with sticky notes, and sometimes fixing things using more optimism than science. Sometimes, all we had was hope, hustle, and a bit of luck. Let's say we learned the hard way: one breakdown at a time.

This book is the result of four decades on the job. I've worked across various industries, including oil and gas, food and beverage, mining, dairy, refining, and transport, on five continents and in places I couldn't have imagined as a young engineer. I've been lost in sugarcane fields in Papua New Guinea, stuck in airports during volcanic eruptions, and nearly kidnapped on a Tunisian train platform.

I've built RCM programs from scratch, introduced Weibull analysis into failure prediction, and survived more than a few cultural mishaps.

I've delivered RCA workshops in Egypt, survived pyramid horse rides, and won a replica rifle at a U.S. conference (and nearly got arrested bringing it home). Every one of those moments, funny, frightening, or frustrating, has shaped what I believe about reliability, leadership, and people.

More than anything, this book is about real practice.

I've seen lubrication programs turn around entire facilities. I've stood in front of site leaders and had to ask for their buy-in because I knew deep down that reliability only works when it starts at the top. I've lived through culture clashes, management indifference, and spreadsheet madness. And still, I've seen what happens when people truly commit. Small wins stack up. Teams begin to trust each other. Reliability becomes a new way of thinking.

Over the years, I've helped implement Reliability in Design, rolled out FMECA-based maintenance strategies, and used tools like Apollo RCA and Isograph AWB to change how companies work. After thousands of site visits, training sessions, breakdowns, and breakthroughs, I realised the most valuable things I've learned weren't tucked away in technical manuals. They came from past conversations, people, mentors, technicians, planners, and operators and from experiences that shaped me, challenged me, and sometimes almost broke me. That's why I wrote this book, and now, I want to share those lessons with you.

WHO IS THIS BOOK FOR?

- The reliability engineer drowning in spreadsheets, chasing recurring failures.
- The maintenance planner wondering why no one sticks to the plan.
- The operator who knows something's off, even when the dashboard is green.
- The maintenance manager juggling cost, performance, and risk like a circus act.
- The apprentice eager to learn, and the veteran still passionate about doing things right.
- The C-suite leader who's just realised that PowerPoint and hope won't keep machines running.

In short, this is for anyone who wants to make things better, safer, and more reliable, no matter your job title or how long you've been in the game.

WHAT'S INSIDE?

This isn't a textbook, and it's not a fairy tale. It's a mix of:

- Stories from the field - some funny, some painful, all real.
- Case studies with insights that are as relevant today as they were when I lived them.
- Overseas survival tips based on a few close calls and cultural missteps.

- Reflections on the people side of reliability - the wins, the frustrations, and the moments that stick with you.
- You'll also find practical advice, reflections on culture, and the occasional survival strategy for when things get really messy (and they will).

WHAT MAKES THIS BOOK DIFFERENT?

This book isn't just about best practice but real practice. It's not written behind a desk or based on a six-month consultancy. It's grounded in over 40 years of real-world experience, with lived global experiences among real people, including real failures and wins, across various industries and continents. It also emphasises human insights because reliability isn't just about machines.

It's about people, process, and purpose.

There are no fluff, magic formulas, or silver bullets here. Just straight talk, human stories, tools, and lessons that have stood the test of time. Just hard-won lessons, honest reflections, and the kind of advice you'd give to a friend on the night shift. Reliability is not just about machines; it's about the people who keep them running and what we can learn from each other when we take the time to listen, reflect, and share.

A NOTE FROM ME

I didn't write this book to impress anyone. I wrote it to give something back and to pass something on. I want to share the lessons I've learned from mentors and teammates, as well as the breakdowns that didn't go as planned. This book is a way to thank the global maintenance and reliability community for the people who've inspired me, challenged me, and kept me learning when things got tough.

If you've ever stayed late to solve a problem that no one else noticed, or if you've ever taken pride in making something run better than it did yesterday, this is for you. I hope you see your own story on some of these pages. I hope you laugh. I hope you pause and reflect. And I hope you walk away with at least one idea, mindset shift, or lesson that makes a difference in your world.

One final ask.... Keep reading. Not only because I want the book to be finished, but because I want these lessons to be used and shared in meetings, training sessions, or toolbox talks, challenge them, debate, and improve them, but don't leave them on the shelf. Because reliability isn't something you achieve once, it's something you build every day. It's a habit. A mindset. A team sport. And if you're still reading, you're probably one of the people who's been quietly improving things all along.
Let's get into it.

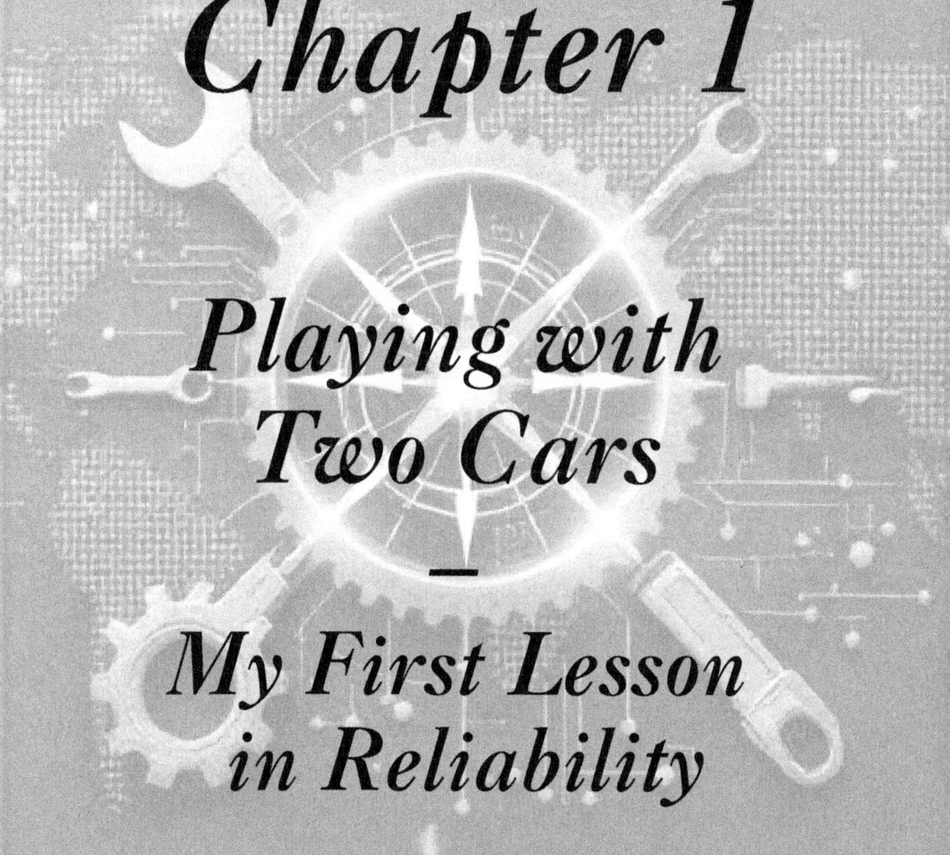

Chapter 1

Playing with Two Cars

—

My First Lesson in Reliability

Playing with Two Cars – My First Lesson in Reliability

"A journey of a thousand miles begins with a single step." Lao Tzu

People often ask me how my journey in reliability began. It all started with a formal apprenticeship, but in reality, it began on a crisp November 19, 1982. I had just turned 14 and started a Saturday job washing trucks at Miles Fox Haulage in Clitheroe, Lancashire. Little did I know that what seemed like a simple weekend gig would unknowingly become the foundation of a lifelong passion.

My task was straightforward: to steam-clean the trucks until they gleamed. These weren't just quick rinses; they had to be spotless, meticulously scrubbed to meet the high standards set by Mr. Fox himself.

You see, Mr. Fox was a man who commanded respect without ever asking for it. He was always working, always moving, always watching. You'd never see him lounging in an office, hidden behind a desk. No, he was in the thick of it, wearing his navy-blue boiler suit and flat cap, cigar clamped between his teeth, barking orders through the thick haze of Sir Henry Wintermans smoke. He smoked as he worked, talked, and thought.

He started with nothing. A council house, a wife, three kids, and one truck. Just one. But that was enough. He built that single truck into a UK national Haulage company that is still operating today, not by luck or shortcuts, but through sheer, unrelenting hard work. And that was the only way he knew how to operate, hands-on, tireless, demanding.

I learned this firsthand with him when I was cleaning his trucks. Mr. Fox himself would inspect my work, and if it wasn't clean enough, there were no shortcuts or excuses; I had to redo it. And again. And again, if necessary, until it met his standards.

One day, after A full day of steam cleaning trucks, what felt like a lifetime's worth of grime, I couldn't hold back my curiosity any longer.

"Mr. Fox," I finally asked, "Why do these trucks need to be so clean? Come Monday, they'll be back in the quarry, covered in dirt again." He stopped, looked me square in the eye, and with a knowing smile, he said something I would never forget:

"When those wheels aren't turning, the trucks aren't earning!"

At the time, it seemed like a simple statement about business efficiency. But there was a more profound lesson buried within those words; one I would only come to fully appreciate later. Cleaning wasn't just for appearance; Dirt and grime could hide potential problems, making it difficult to spot leaks, defects, cracks, or mechanical wear. The trucks needed to be spotless so mechanics could spot minor issues before they became major problems.

Mr. Fox went on to explain how a careful eye and a bit of elbow grease could save a company time, thousands of pounds in breakdowns and repairs, and effort in the long run. He expected everyone around him to live by that same philosophy.

He was quite a character, a force of nature, gruff, sharp, and as unyielding as the steel of his trucks. If things weren't done right, if standards slipped, you'd know about it. He had a temper, not wild or reckless, but fierce and undeniable. He never directed it at me, but I'd seen him lose patience when things didn't go his way.

That was Mr. Fox's way. Hard work. Attention to detail. Prevention over cure. And above all else, an unshakable belief that:

"If you work hard, you'll get the results, and you'll get the life that you want!"

THE £5 TEST

On my first weekend, after working Friday evening and all day Saturday, Mr Fox took me to the office and pulled out his wallet, which was full of crisp £5, £10, and £20 notes. I was about to get my first wage.

And guess what it would be?

Mr Fox handed me a crisp £5 note. I was probably expecting more, but it was my first weekend after all. When I got home, my Mum and Dad asked me how things had gone. I showed them my first-ever money that I had worked hard for - the fresh, crisp £5 note. My Mum wasn't impressed and said I had been underpaid. My Dad asked if I had enjoyed it, and I said I had, that I had really enjoyed it. When I returned the following weekend and followed the same ritual, Mr Fox took me to the office for payment. This time, I received £20.

He said, "I only paid you £5 last week because I wanted to see if you would return because of the money or if you wanted to work for me."

I had been tested, and I'm so glad that I did return. Although I didn't realise it then, Mr. Fox was planting the seed of a philosophy that would shape my entire career: Reliability isn't just about fixing things when they break; it's about preventing them from breaking in the first place.

I was being introduced to a world where the smallest overlooked detail could mean the difference between a smooth operation and a costly breakdown. More importantly, he was teaching me about the mindset of reliability!

From that moment on, I saw the job differently. I wasn't just washing trucks; I was learning how machines lived and aged. You see, that job at Miles Fox Haulage was more than just a Saturday job; it was the beginning of a journey. A journey that began with a bucket of soapy water and a high-pressure steam cleaner ultimately shaped my perspective on the world. Because in life, much like in mechanics:

"If you look after your equipment, it will look after you"

I was fortunate that my job didn't stop at washing trucks. Initially, I had to focus on getting the basics right. My main task was to clean the vehicles, but as time passed, I was allowed to step into the garage, where I began to learn the fundamentals of truck maintenance. It was a hands-on education like no other. I learned tasks on truck services, including fluid level checks, lubrication, tyre pressures, and tread depth checks, as well as performing oil and filter changes. I even got to help with tyre replacements and other essential maintenance tasks.

For a kid eager to learn, it was like being handed the keys to a secret world. I soaked up knowledge like a sponge, hands covered in grease, heart racing with excitement. It never felt like work. It was great fun, and I was fortunate to have gained so much practical experience at such a young age.
However, the truth is that, as I sit here writing this book and reflecting on my journey, I realise my path to reliability began even earlier than I had given it credit for, around 1975.

Of course, at the time, I had no idea. I was just a seven-year-old kid, more interested in getting my hands dirty than in understanding the bigger picture.

THE DAY I LEARNED WHY TWO IS BETTER THAN ONE

Our family car was a pale blue Hillman Imp, a small but characterful little thing that Dad treated as a prized possession. We didn't have a fancy garage; we had a simple, rented wooden one behind our house. Every time Dad serviced our car, or as soon as he lifted the bonnet, I was right there beside him, watching, learning, and, most importantly, getting stuck in. He always allowed me to help, and he taught me the basics of the internal combustion engine in a way that made perfect sense to my seven-year-old brain. It wasn't just about fixing cars, I loved everything about it: the thrill of getting my hands mucky and that strong, heady smell of oil lingering long after we'd finished.

And now, looking at my son, I can see where he gets this desire for being a muck magnet! It must be in the genes.

One of my absolute greatest childhood thrills was when Dad allowed me to sit on his knee and "drive" the car along the back street. To me, it was pure magic. The feeling of the steering wheel beneath my small hands, the gentle hum of the engine, the way the car moved as if I were the one in control, it was exhilarating. I felt like a proper driver, like I was doing something incredibly grown-up. Mum, however, was far less impressed. The moment she found out, well, let's say that particular adventure came to an abrupt and permanent end. She wasn't having any of it. Mum said it was too risky, and just like that, my short-lived career as a seven-year-old driver was over.

Then came the Saturday morning that's still etched in my memory. Dad announced that he'd rented a second garage. "For a new car, a second Hillman Imp," he said.

"A new car?", I blurted out.

This was big news!Well, it was new to us. Because Dad never bought a brand-new car. Not then, not ever. Even to this day, he's never purchased a brand-new car. "You lose too much money the minute you drive them out of the showroom," he'd say, shaking his head at the thought, "A waste of money".

That way of thinking has stuck with me over the years, although I have had a couple of brand-new cars in my life, I couldn't help but lean toward Dad's philosophy. There's a certain logic to it that makes sense. Why take the financial hit when I could wait for the purchasing of something with the initial depreciation losses removed? By the time I buy a car, the worst of that drop in value has already happened, making the overall cost of ownership much more manageable.

I still remember the day when the car delivery truck arrived. I'd expected excitement, maybe even the usual flurry of revving engines, but instead, the Hillman Imp was carefully unloaded and then, much to my confusion, pushed into the garage because it was a non-runner.

I was puzzled. "Dad, why do we have two?" I asked, frowning at the lifeless vehicle now sitting beside our old one.

Dad wiped his hands on a rag and explained, "We're soon driving to Minehead for a summer holiday at Butlins, a 500-mile round trip. Our current Hillman Imp was starting to show issues and had broken down a few times already.

"Can't trust it for a big trip like this. So, this one here," he gestured to the new arrival, still looking sorry for itself in the garage, "This one is backup. Redundancy, in case the main one fails."

I didn't understand it in those terms back then, but looking back, it was my first real encounter with "reliability in action." It wasn't just about cars; it was about thinking ahead, having a safety net. In Dad's world, you didn't wait for things to go wrong before making a plan. You prepared for the worst, so you weren't caught off guard when it happened.

At the time, though, I was less interested in life lessons. I was too busy wondering whether this so-called "backup" car would actually start or if we were building a collection of broken vehicles.

Over the next few weekends, Dad and I worked side by side, swapping parts from the "out of service" pale green Imp, now officially retired, to the roadworthy light blue Imp, preparing it for the road trip. It was our little project and another reason for Dad and me to spend hours together, elbow-deep in oil and grease, lost in our little world of engines and spanners.

Then came the big moment: we finally took it out on the A59 for a test drive, half-excited, half-nervous, and I braced myself for rattles, coughs, maybe even the whole thing giving up halfway. But to my surprise, it ran beautifully, without a single rattle.

And when the real test came, the long drive to Minehead!

Well, it passed with flying colours.

Not only did it get us to Minehead and back without a hitch, but it also securely held all our luggage on the roof rack.

Although we soon realised that the Imp wasn't the best size for a family of four, Dad's love for Hillman cars didn't fade. It wasn't long before we upgraded to a larger, more practical car: a bronze Hillman Hunter. I can still picture it, gleaming under the streetlights, its registration MRN 145J. It felt like a proper car, bigger, sturdier, a step up from the tiny Imp.

But, of course, Dad wasn't one to stick with just one Hunter. Soon, another came along, another pale-yellow Hunter, MBV 757P. And then, after that, a white Talbot Alpine, AJX 916V. The driveway was never empty for long; as soon as one car left, another would roll in, needing some care and attention.

Eventually, Dad moved on to Fords and Vauxhalls. Strangely enough, despite the years that have passed, I can still remember every single registration number of those old cars as if they were etched into my brain.

Meanwhile, my current car's plate? Completely escapes me half the time. I even entered it wrong last year while paying the Dartford crossing toll, only to receive a fine in the post!

Reflecting on all this, I realise that my introduction to reliability didn't start in 1982, but rather in 1975, in our driveway, with Dad teaching me concepts I didn't even know I was learning, such as redundancy, uptime, availability, lubrication, and precision maintenance.

Back then, it wasn't about engineering terms; it was simply about ensuring the car would start in the morning, about knowing how to listen for the right noises and identify the wrong ones.

And so, at the age of seven, my journey of reliability began...

Chapter 2

Early Sparks of Engineering

Early Sparks of Engineering

"It is not in the stars to hold our destiny but in ourselves."
William Shakespeare

I was always more of a hands-on, practical kind of kid. Sitting in a classroom all day just wasn't my thing. I loved being creative with my hands, whether it was building something, fixing things, or just figuring stuff out. I wasn't the studious type, and honestly, I didn't really enjoy my time in junior school. Looking back, though, I can see how even the little moments, like fixing a puncture, noticing a teacher's car gleaming in the sunlight, or feeling out of place at a desk, were quietly shaping me.

This chapter is about those sparks, the early experiences that planted the seeds of curiosity, resilience, and problem-solving that would eventually guide me toward engineering and reliability.

FINDING MY FLOW

Back then, my junior school primarily focused on the clever kids and those who had a chance of passing their 11+ exam and gaining admission to the local Grammar School.

That was the big goal, and if you weren't on that path, well, you were left behind. I failed my 11+ and even at a young age, I felt like I'd already been stamped with the label "failure." Not a great feeling for a kid, to be honest.

But outside the classroom? That's where I came alive. I preferred to be out playing on my bike, which I had had a few over my younger years. First, a Raleigh Grifter, then a Chopper, and eventually my pride and joy: my first, Eddie Merckx special road racing bike.

One bike I always wanted but I was never allowed was a BMX because Mum didn't want me doing stunts and risking hurting myself. Yes, she would tell me the likelihood of an accident increased on a BMX because they were designed for performing stunts and since I wasn't trained to be a stunt rider, the risk of injury was too high. Looking back, that was my earliest introduction to risk management, if you can believe it! The risk was injury, and Mum was the risk assessor. Funny thing is, if only she had seen what I could do on my Grifter!

I didn't just ride my bike; I also loved working on it, fixing punctures, repairing broken chains, and adjusting brakes, among other tasks. That was the fun bit for me. I enjoyed getting my hands dirty and figuring things out. It felt good to fix something with my own two hands.

Sadly, my Eddie Merckx was eventually written off in an accident after my dad borrowed it to cycle to work. He left it in the yard at his workplace, and it got run over by a truck. It wasn't anyone's fault, really; it was just one of those random accidents. I suppose that was the bike's final moment, its "end-of-life disposal," you could say.

I turned 11, and it was time to move on to secondary school. I ended up at a small school tucked away in the countryside called Bowland County Secondary School, though most of us affectionately knew it as 'Riversmead'. That name had a charm to it, and honestly, so did the school itself. This was where things started to change for me, for the better. This is where I began to thrive. Riversmead felt like a fresh start. The atmosphere was completely different from junior school. It was warm, encouraging, and felt like a place where everyone mattered.

It felt like the school wanted everyone to succeed in life. I made some great friends here. No one was made to feel like a failure here, and for the first time, I felt like I belonged.

Mr Crossley, our headmaster and huge rugby fan, was also a fan of classic cars, something that I also ended up having a passion for. But what caught my attention was his love for classic cars. He drove to school in an old Daimler Sovereign, and he also had an old Wolseley. And he wasn't the only one!

One of the other teachers, Mrs Malone, also drove to school in her white Triumph Stag. Those cars were very well maintained, always spotless, polished like mirrors, and looked after with love.

I was fascinated. I couldn't help but notice the little details, the chrome finishes, and the engine sounds. Aside from admiring the cars, I enjoyed the rugby. I loved the physical challenge and the team spirit. Athletics was significant, too. I enjoyed pushing myself to see how far or fast I could go. But it wasn't just sports that grabbed my interest. I also started to enjoy most of my classes. Geography was one of my favourite subjects, and the idea of global travel was always on my mind.

In my final year, something extraordinary happened. I was privileged to be asked to be the school deputy Head Boy and also captain of our rugby team and vice-captain of our school society 'Walker' – That felt like a huge deal. I felt proud, not just because of the titles, but because I knew I'd come a long way from that kid who felt like a failure after the 11+. I enjoyed this school.

Riversmead wasn't just a regular school for me. It was the place that lit a fire within me, helping shape who I was becoming. It showed me that success looks different for everyone, and that with the right support, you can find your path. It really did set me off on my journey into the big, wide world.

THE ARMY DETOUR

So, there I was, standing at a crossroads, thinking about my future and what path to take. I considered joining the army. Not just any part of it, though, I had a dream to get into the Royal Electrical and Mechanical Engineers (REME). My cousin Michael was in this division, and he was someone I looked up to. He was a bit of a legend in our family. He even made it into the Guinness Book of Records for the maximum number of sit-ups in 24 hours. What an achievement! I was super proud of him and wanted to follow in his footsteps.

I filled out the army application, and soon I was invited for a weekend of training and recruitment at a location called Sutton Coalfield in the Midlands, UK. I was buzzing with excitement. That weekend was packed with 'army' activities, think obstacle courses, team tasks, early mornings, and lots of marching. It was tough, but I loved every minute of it. At the end of the weekend, I was thrilled to find out that I had passed the selection. It felt like I was one step closer to my dream.

However, whilst I was successful in selection for the 'army', unfortunately, my choice of joining the REME suffered a blow. During the medical checks, they discovered I was colour blind, and due to the electrical work requirements, I was seen as unfit to perform those duties.

As a result, I wasn't allowed to join REME. Gutted doesn't even begin to cover it. It was like someone had pulled the plug on my big plan. Doh! Back to the drawing board. I didn't let this setback get me down for too long, though.

APPRENTICESHIP

I picked myself up and started applying for engineering apprenticeships in industry, and I was offered two interviews. One at the local Cement works 'Ribblesdale Cement (now owned by Heidelberg) and another at ICI Agricultural Catalyst Division (now owned by Johnson Matthey).

I attended both the interviews and was fortunate to be offered both positions. The role was the same for each: 'Apprentice Mechanical Maintenance Technician'. My first thought was to go with Ribblesdale since my dad worked for the cement company, and this seemed the logical choice. However, after a good chat with my dad, we decided that an apprenticeship with ICI (a global chemical company and one of the largest companies in the world) would put me in good standing for the future and other opportunities.

"Think long term," he said.

He was right. And so, after receiving my offer of a position at ICI, I gladly signed the offer and officially began my apprenticeship on August 12, 1985.

Funny enough, August 12 is known as the "Glorious Twelfth" in the UK and is the start of the grouse shooting season. As luck would have it, my mentor and I were away shooting for the day on my first day. His name was Rodney Bury, and he quickly became a huge influence on me. What a guy. In those early days, he taught me so much, especially when it came to working with tools and doing things properly.

One of the first lessons was about the importance of lubrication. Rodney was meticulous about ensuring everything was properly greased. Everything was rebuilt with a generous coating of copper slip, to the point where we jokingly started calling it 'Rodney slip'. Nothing ever seized after Rodney had overhauled it. If he overhauled a part, you could be sure that it would run smoothly for years. He was one of those people who made a lasting impression, and a lot of what I learned from him stuck with me ever since.

I had to go through an induction week before moving into the workshops to meet the engineering team and my new colleagues. The induction was predominantly focused on health and safety, and soon I realised that I was working in a dangerous facility with some nasty chemicals. The risks were very real. One moment from that induction has stayed with me forever. Mr Flynn, the induction trainer, walked in one morning holding a small bag from the Butcher's. Inside were real 'bull's eyes'. Yep, actual eyeballs. We all looked at each other like, "What on earth is going on here?"

He went ahead and showed us what a few drops of 'caustic soda' could do to an eyeball. I was almost sick. But you know what? That shocking demo did precisely what it was meant to do: it got the message across loud and clear. Those early health and safety inductions have stuck with me throughout my career. I will always be grateful to ICI for that; it provided me with a solid foundation and instilled in me a deep respect for doing things the right way. It also became clear to me early on that safety and reliability go hand in hand.

The culture that drives safety also drives reliability, valuing good maintenance, proper planning, and doing things once and doing them right. That mindset has stuck with me and become a significant part of how I've approached reliability ever since.

The ICI plant was a fantastic learning ground that provided me with great hands-on experience in maintenance, reliability, learning, and understanding.

The apprenticeship was excellent. It was the complete package. It covered all aspects of engineering, from pipefitting, welding, machining, and fitting, to overhauls, installations, and even some design work. It was proper, solid training that delivered everything you needed to know. For someone like me, fresh out of school and eager to learn, it was exactly what I was looking for.

WAKE-UP CALLS IN MAINTENANCE

One thing that stood out at ICI was the seriousness with which they took safety. The site was kept legal and compliant, and safety was paramount in everything we did or at least everything that had to be compliant by law. That's where things started to get a bit confusing for me. Unfortunately, the equipment that didn't fall under legal compliance was often left in what they'd call a "run to fail" condition. If it wasn't required by law to be maintained, it was used until it broke. No planning, no regular upkeep, just wait until it fails, then scramble to fix it. It was something I struggled with. I couldn’t help thinking,

“Why could these assets fail so often, and why was nobody asking 'why'?"

Coming from my time working with Mr Fox at the haulage company, I’d seen what proper routine maintenance looked like. There were routine servicing, including greasing, oil changes, and brake adjustments, among others, and I witnessed some very well-maintained trucks. But here I was now, at ICI – the ‘World Class’ chemical company. Well, I was watching pumps, valves, motors, gearboxes, basically everything breaking down left, right, and centre. And when they failed, it would then be a panic. Everyone is rushing to repair, especially if the issue occurred during a critical production run.

But I then realised all production runs were "critical." There was never a “good” time for something to fail, yet no one seemed interested in preventing those failures in the first place.

I learned about something called 'Preventive Maintenance' in college, which involves performing small, regular tasks to keep equipment healthy and prevent major breakdowns. It just made sense to me. So, I mentioned it a few times to our Engineering Manager. I explained that by performing regular maintenance tasks, such as servicing, checking oil levels, replacing worn parts, and inspecting for wear and tear, we could prevent many of these failures. But no one seemed to be listening. They did not show much interest.

It was all reactive, fixing things when they broke. That was frustrating, especially when I could see a better way. I didn't have all the answers back then, but I knew that doing nothing until something failed wasn’t the right approach either.

Around that time, ICI underwent significant global changes. The Clitheroe site, where I was based, ended up getting partnered with another facility over in the United States, a catalyst plant just outside Chicago. With that partnership, came a new name: called ICI Katalco. It wasn’t long after the rebranding that the Chicago plant was closed and all of its production was transferred to ICI Katalco's Clitheroe facility.

And that's when the 'reliability' fun began.

Technically, the Clitheroe plant had the capacity to take on the Chicago orders for catalysts. On paper, it looked doable. But in reality, we didn't have the availability, and that's because we were still operating in a classic "run to failure" mode. Things broke, and we fixed them.

Running equipment to failure is expensive, costing 3 to 10 times more than preventive maintenance. However, ICI was cash-rich; nobody considered the cost of being unreliable. But, with production capacity set to double, the run-to-failure approach was no longer viable.

That moment became a turning point for me. That's when my first real opportunity arose to step away from Maintenance and get involved in something bigger. I became seconded into an ICI organisation called 'Manufacturing Technology', a kind of internal team focused on improving how we do things. That's where I got to learn all about the reliability tools and methods: RCM (Reliability Centred Maintenance), FMECA (Failure Modes, Effects and Criticality Analysis), RCA (Root Cause Analysis), TPM (Total Productive Maintenance), CBM (Condition-Based Maintenance), you name it. All the acronyms that are still around to this day, 30 years later!

I was lucky enough to work alongside some excellent engineers who taught me a great deal...It was also at this time that I was introduced to a gentleman named Ron Moore, a true guru in the world of manufacturing and reliability. He was based in the USA and had already built a solid reputation for his no-nonsense approach to improving plant performance. I was able to get a copy of his book Making Common Sense Common Practice. I still have the book on my shelf and got it signed by Ron a few years later. It was my go-to Bible for Manufacturing Excellence.

Ron had been doing some consulting work with ICI for a while by then. He had visited several sites and had taken a good look under the bonnet, and for the American readers, I am referring to the 'hood', so to speak. After gathering all his findings, he was able to present them back to the ICI board of directors. ICI was an old-school British business. A traditional British giant. It carried that "Best of British" pride and, let's be honest, a fair bit of snobbery too. Back then, ICI were number one in the FTSE index. They were the company to work for, and everyone wanted to be like ICI; they thought they were invincible.

Then came Ron's feedback.

He stood in front of the board and delivered one of the boldest statements, 'You have allowed Mediocrity to become your Standard for Best Practice, " he told the ICI Board of Directors. Boom!

The reaction? Let's say they were not happy!

How dare this 'Yank' come over here and start telling ICI, the best of British industry, that we are mediocre? But here's the thing... he was spot on. ICI was mediocre. On the surface, we appeared to be a world-class organisation. The numbers, the reputation, the branding, they all looked impressive. But underneath, we were firefighting, letting equipment fail, ignoring preventable problems, and clinging to old ways of working. We were surviving, not improving.

Ron didn't stop there. He warned the board that if ICI did not change the way it did business, it would no longer exist as a company.

And well... where is ICI today? Exactly. It's gone.

The company that once stood at the top of the FTSE, that proudly carried the famous roundel, is now just a memory. Over time, it was split up, sold off in pieces, and absorbed into other companies. That iconic ICI brand, once the symbol of British industrial might, was gone forever.

Looking back, it's sad, really. There was so much potential, with many great people and a rich legacy. But the world changed, and ICI didn't change fast enough. Ron saw it coming. He tried to warn them. And unfortunately, he was right.

Fast forward to me, stepping into my new role, it was clear: the challenge was set. The task was simple in words, but not in practice: identify the losses in time, money, and efficiency, pareto them, and start to eliminate them one by one. I remember when we measured our plant's availability for the first time, it was at 50%. That was a shock. We needed to reach at least 80%. Why? Because we were about to take on extra production from the US plant that had recently shut down. They were relying on us to pick up the slack and keep everything running smoothly.

So, we rolled up our sleeves and got to work. We established several groups called 'Manufacturing Improvement Teams' (MITs), and each team targeted a number of specific, small projects aimed at eliminating losses and increasing plant uptime.

One of our biggest and most frustrating production losses was being 'caused by' (a phrase I would later become very familiar with) a regular failure of a Worthington Simpson centrifugal pump, specifically pump number 3J24. This pump was operating on a soda carbonate transfer system, and, unfortunately, it was a single point of failure. In simpler terms, if it went down, everything stopped. This would result in immediate losses in plant production. That pump wasn't just a piece of equipment anymore; it became my personal mission. In fact, that was my MIT project.

So now, I had to put some of my recent training to the test.

One of the challenges at ICI was trying to determine the cost per hour of failure. It turned out that the business did not want the site employees to know how much profit the plant was making. This number would then be used by the unions when it came to wage rise discussions, or by competitors in the industry. It was understandable why this number was unknown, but without understanding the financial impact on production losses, we could not determine whether some things should be maintained or indeed let them run to failure.

Understanding the cost of an asset failure per hour in a production plant is critically important because it gives you a clear financial lens on the true impact of downtime, far beyond just the repair bill. Knowing the cost helps:

- Quantify the Pain
- Prioritises the Maintenance Effort
- Justifies Investment
- Drives Better Decision Making
- Supports Better Scheduling

Understanding the cost per hour of failure enables maintenance to transition from a cost centre to a value generator.

It moves the conversation from "How much does maintenance cost?" to "How much value does it protect?"

So eventually, after many discussions and debates, it was agreed that a cost would be issued, and that cost was given as £4360 per hour of revenue loss.

The losses were quantified, and the plan was to start with a facilitated Root Cause Analysis (RCA) investigation. I assembled a small team, and we began creating the cause-and-effect chart. We also had some standard tools ready, such as the 5 Whys and Fishbone diagram. But then, I decided this warranted a more in-depth examination. It wasn't just a textbook exercise; this was real, messy, and it directly affected people and performance.

As my career in reliability took off, I quickly learned that not every tool is suitable for every job. I soon realised that Fishbone (Ishikawa diagram) and 5 Whys were not always the right tools for the situation. I always found the fishbone diagram to be too much of a guessing tool, and while the 5 Whys worked for simple issues, it was too linear, especially when problems became complex. It's like trying to fix a puzzle with just one piece.

This early frustration with these RCA tools? It hit me even harder during my first week working in New Zealand in 2001, but I'll delve into that story later in the book, and trust me, it's worth the wait. Anyway, the RCA was completed (you can review the full report on the next page), and the solutions we implemented were effective.

ROOT CAUSE ANALYSIS REPORT		**Report Ref No**
Equipment Number 3J24	**Equipment Name** Soda Carbonate Pump	**Date** April 1997
Date of Failure(s) Dec 95 – Apr 97	**Downtime Production Loss** 88 Hours	**Owner** G Tyne

Problem Statement

3J24 Pump is continually failing and has experienced 22 mechanical seal failures in 16 months. This pump is critical to production and runs 24/7, when this pump fails total production is lost.

Impact Statement

Cost of failure:

Labour = 88 hours @ £13/hr = £1144

Parts = £8052

Revenue Loss:

88 hours @ £4360 per hour = £383,680

Safety:

Potential risk of injury during unplanned maintenance activity

Reliability:

MTBF = 530 Hours MTTR = 4 Hours

The Analysis - 5W FB CF (highlight analysis type)

The RCA team were brought together and a Causal Factors chart was developed to determine the root causes of pump failure.

Post-Its were used on a wall and we started with the 'Pump Failure' as our key cause.

Through the development of the causal factors chart and team discussions, several root causes were identified along with supporting evidence. Subsequent solutions were identified to prevent any further pump failures and increase the MTBF.

The Mechanical seal manufacturer was invited to the RCA and they provided evidence from previous seal failures

Solutions

Cause	Solution	Name	Due Date
Back Pressure on Mech Seal due to incorrect sizing of kickback line	Resize and replace kickback line and associated valves.		
Overheating of Mech Seal due to direct steam flush	Replace direct steam flush for thermosyphon and cooling fin arrangement		
Vibration of Mech Seal due to loose bed plate and damaged concrete plinth	Repair the concrete pump plinth and secure bed plate.		
Vibration of Mech Seal due to no alignment policy	Perform laser alignment policy on pump/motor		

Success Tracking – 6M – 12M – 24M (highlight failure free period)

All four solutions were implemented and visual monitoring of the pump and thermosyphon was carried out on a weekly basis initially for the first 3 months, followed by monthly checks.

The solutions were costed and a payback period of 3 months were achieved.

The pump ran for 11 months and 25 days before the first defect was identified.

The inner seal of the double seal had failed and product was seen within the thermosyphon sight glass. This was an early warning of failure and allowed us to stop the pump and replace the seal during the next planned outage.

The pump continued to operate with a new MTBF = 8030 hours.

It really worked. The pump, which had experienced 22 failures in 16 months, finally ran for 11 months and 25 days without any further failures. And when it did finally fail, it wasn't some catastrophic breakdown. The failure was detected by visual check, and no unplanned downtime was incurred.

That moment was a game-changer for me. This was my first real RCA, and I was sold on the process. We didn't stop there. We also did an RCM study on that same pump and its surrounding valves and instruments, all considered within their actual operating context and boundaries. I was up and running and thoroughly enjoying this personal journey of reliability and discovery. It wasn't just about the pump anymore; it was about understanding the whole system. And you know what? I loved it.

It was me, and this is what I wanted to do. I had finally found my passion. It felt like I was on a personal journey, one full of learning, problem-solving, and discovery. It reminded me of being a kid again, when I had the passion for my dad's Hillman Imps, tinkering with the trucks at Mr Fox's haulage company, and fixing up my bicycles at home. Back then, I didn't have a name for it. But here, at this moment, standing next to the 3J24 pump. I still remember it; I had a moment of absolute clarity. Yes, that was the moment when I truly realised I'd found my passion. Reliability was my destiny.

BEARINGS AND BREAKDOWN BATTLES

Not long after, we also experienced a large failure of a compactor gearbox onsite – labelled 4L1. And not just a minor issue, either; it was a major breakdown. It was right in the middle of a production campaign and really could not have happened at a worse time. Production pressures had intensified, and to make things even more stressful, we had no backup stock of the required catalysts. Everything was being made just in time, to order. There was no room for delays.

We rushed to do an initial assessment. It didn't take long to realise how serious it was. The gearbox had essentially seized, and upon opening it, we found missing teeth on the gears. This wasn't a quick fix. To make things even more complicated, this gearbox had been running for years, since the building was built. In fact, the building was built around the gearbox, making it almost impossible to remove.

But we didn't give up. We rallied two full breakdown teams working 24/7. Everyone pulled together. It was one of those intense moments where you see what your team is really made of. I was tasked with supervising the rebuild, and at the same time, I had to start collecting evidence for the RCA, which we planned to do after production was back up and running.

I was running on adrenaline, switching between helping the team troubleshoot, coordinating with suppliers, and snapping photos or jotting down notes for the RCA. It felt like being in the middle of a storm, chaotic and high-stakes, but somehow, there was also a strange kind of energy that pushed us through.

To make things even trickier, we had no technical drawings of the gearbox; it was an old, obsolete model. And, to top it off, the original manufacturer was no longer in business. It felt like we were flying blind.

Still, we've got to work it out. We stripped the gearbox down piece by piece, trying to figure out exactly what we needed. It turned out we needed to get new bearings, a shaft repair and some new gears to be manufactured. Not exactly an easy shopping list.

Our local bearing supplier, the one we'd always used, was able to locate some bearings. Unfortunately, they told us these were in the USA and would need to be flown across as an urgent delivery. To be honest, I wasn't thrilled about that. During my reliability journey at ICI, my confidence in this local bearing supplier was often tested, and it is fair to say I did not trust them. I had raised concerns on several occasions (which could be another chapter in this book!), but management overlooked them. I guess management didn't want to rock the boat.

Anyway, the bearings arrived a few days later. We were all waiting anxiously, and when I finally opened the shipment, I was expecting to see clean, fresh components packed carefully and ready to go. But that was when I got a shock.

Upon inspection, I could see that these bearings were second-hand, old bearings that had been supplied. The grease-proof paper had decayed, and some of the boxes were not even original. I remember just sitting there for a moment, stunned. I felt like we'd been cheated and worse, like we'd just lost more valuable time on a job that couldn't afford delays.

This was not good. Frustrated, I immediately picked up the phone and contacted the local supplier. I told them the bearings they had delivered were second-hand and in worse condition than the ones we had removed. I was told there were no other available anywhere in the world. I contacted the bearing manufacturer, which was something you didn't do in the UK; you had to deal with bearing suppliers. But I'd had enough. I picked up the phone and contacted the bearing manufacturer myself.

To my surprise, the manufacturer was excellent and incredibly helpful. They arrived promptly and inspected the bearings we'd received. After checking them, the inspector confirmed what I already suspected.

"These," he said, holding one up, "were installed on an old mill machine from a site in Birmingham. These aren't from the US, they're from the UK. And they're 19 years old."

"Wait, what?" I asked, stunned. "Nineteen years old?"
"Yes", he nodded. "They're even older than the ones you removed."

I couldn't believe it. Well, that was it. There was no way I was going to install bearings nearly two decades old. Thankfully, the bearing manufacturer was able to locate some in a warehouse in Manchester, brand new bearings as we had expected.

So, while our local supplier was charging for international shipping from the USA, these bearings had been located in the UK all along. I knew I'd have to address that later, but right now I had bigger problems to deal with. I had to inform the Engineering Manager of a further delay, approximately 12 hours, due to the bearings not being fit for purpose and requiring the relocation of additional bearings. The Engineering Manager was not impressed at all and ordered me to install these second-hand bearings, but I refused.

"I can't do that," I replied firmly and explained. "They're second-hand and in poor condition. They won't last. We'll be right back in the same situation again in a few weeks, maybe sooner."

He raised his voice, clearly losing patience. "Just get on and install them!"

That's when I'd had enough. I looked at him and said, "If you want those bearings installed, you'll have to do it yourself. I'm not putting my name on this."

He stared at me, stunned. I decided to illustrate the point with an example.

"Let me ask you something," I said. "You drive a Honda, right?"
"Yes," he replied, a bit confused. "Why?"
"Because it's a strong, reliable car," I continued.
"Now imagine if your wheel bearing collapsed and the local Honda dealer offered to replace the bearing with one in worse condition, and charge full price for the service, would you accept that?"
He paused. "No. Of course not."
"Well," I said calmly, "then I rest my case."

He didn't say another word. We waited for the new bearings to arrive from the warehouse in Manchester. The hours ticked by slowly, and everyone on the team was on edge. No one wanted to lose more time, but at least we knew proper bearings were finally on the way. Once they arrived, we got on with the installation.

But unfortunately, the delay had already taken its toll. The plant lost three weeks of production, and the customer didn't receive their bulk load of catalyst on time.

Once things were up and running again, it was time to look at what had gone wrong. In my role focusing on reliability, I knew we needed more than just a fix; we needed to understand 'why' this happened. So, with all the evidence in hand, and in my reliability role, I facilitated an RCA. We identified several root causes along with solutions.

- Bearing seized due to a lack of lubrication
- Top gearbox misalignment
- Compactor Operation – reworking pellets through the compactor
- Hydraulic pressures are being altered while the machine is running
- Reset timer being overridden

With production up and running, I then addressed the procurement issues with the local bearing supplier. What had happened was unacceptable, and I wanted answers. I booked a meeting, presented the facts, and even brought photos and documentation. However, to my disappointment, the management was not interested. I could not convince them that we needed to change suppliers. It was at this point that I realised I was fighting a losing battle. I was the Lone Ranger on the reliability front.

Everyone else was content just to fix what broke, slap a bandage on it, and move on. All the staff who had worked tirelessly through the three-week turnaround were invited to the conference room (including me). The Engineering Manager was there to thank everyone for their efforts in resolving this situation as quickly as possible. We were all given a voucher as a gift to a local restaurant, where we could take our partners for a meal.

I looked down at the voucher in my hand and felt... conflicted. Sure, the gesture was nice. But something about it didn't sit right. Here we were being presented with a reward for fixing a failure that should never have happened in the first place. And that bothered me. So, in front of the group, I spoke up.

"This is great," I said, "But we are being rewarded for failure. We should never have been in this situation to begin with."

The room fell silent. The Engineering Manager looked at me and asked,

"Do you want to hand your voucher back then?"

Anyway, I kept my voucher, but this wasn't helping drive reliability improvement; in fact, it was encouraging the opposite. The site didn't want reliable systems.

They just wanted superheroes in capes and wearing their underwear on the outside and saving the day.

Reliability is silent when it works; machines run, production targets are met, teams operate without stress, and customers are happy. There are no alarms, no chaos and no emergency meetings. Everyone assumes this is just ‘business as usual’

But when reliability fails, the plant is in crisis mode, managers are scrambling, customers get informed, fingers start being pointed, and everyone asks the same question: “Why wasn't this prevented?”

One thing I was also starting to realise at ICI was how important site leadership is to the reliability journey. And now, even more so today, I know it's absolutely pivotal to its success. Without visible, consistent support from the top, even the best technical strategies will struggle to gain traction.

Site leadership drives the reliability journey by turning strategy into action, aligning people and priorities and creating the culture where reliability can thrive.

A LEAP OF FAITH

And so, whilst my journey continued at ICI for a couple more years, something inside me had started to shift. The constant, overbearing weight of trying to drive reliability improvements had become too much and had slowly worn me down. So, after 15 years of loyal service, I decided my journey with ICI had come to an end. I needed to get out and see the world.

That wasn't just a random thought. It had been growing inside me for years, since I was 20 years old. A moment in time I'll never forget. You see, during my time at ICI in my early 20s, my world turned upside down when my Mum was diagnosed with lung cancer. She had been ill for several months before we got the diagnosis. Her last three weeks of life were both heartbreaking and strangely beautiful.

I was lucky enough to be there with her. I got to sit with Mum and chat about life, the future, and what that might bring. One day she turned to me, using her nickname for me with a soft smile, she said something I've never forgotten, 'Don't hang around here Spud, there's nothing here, get yourself to Australia, see the world and enjoy life', and whilst I agreed with her, I did not have any intention of moving away at that time. I couldn't even picture it. I was rooted where I was, my friends were here, my job, my life.

Australia felt like a postcard fantasy, not a real option. And besides, how could I just pack up and go when everything I knew was right here?

But as my time at ICI passed, I started to feel a restlessness growing inside me. I wanted something different, so I started looking for adventure. Then one day in 1996, I saw an advert in the national newspaper 'Bob Skeleton Racers Required'.

I chuckled to myself. "This sounds like a challenge," I thought.

I have always loved winter sports, and I have been skiing since the age of 11. So, hurtling down some ice on nothing more than a tray - well, yes, that sounds like fun.

I applied for a position and, after going through a selection process, I was selected, along with 14 other novices, to head to Norway for Bob Skeleton trials. I couldn't believe it.

"This is really happening", I thought.

We flew out to Lillehammer, the home of the 1994 Winter Olympics, and arrived in a snow-covered wonderland. After a good night's sleep, we were taken to look at the bobsleigh track. It was massive. Twisting curves, steep drops, high walls of ice, it was amazing.

We were given our sledges and helmets and put to the test. I still remember that first run, the anticipation at the top of the track. The instructor gave us the nod. The cold air fills my lungs. And then, whoosh, off I went. Even to this day, nothing compares to that feeling as a run down the ice on a bob skeleton at 80kmph with your chin almost touching the ice!!

Honestly, it was the most exhilarating experience of my life. Until day three.

We were picking up speed with every run, getting braver. Maybe too brave. Unfortunately for me, my chin did touch the ice on day 3 of the racing, and along with a bump to the head, some stitches, my bob skeleton career and bid for Olympic glory were over. But you know what? I have no regrets. The memory would be with me forever.

Fast forward ten years after my mum passed and after being ICI for 15 years, my mum's words from all those years ago came back to me again, clearer than ever. I was looking for a new challenge and wanted to see the world and do some travelling.

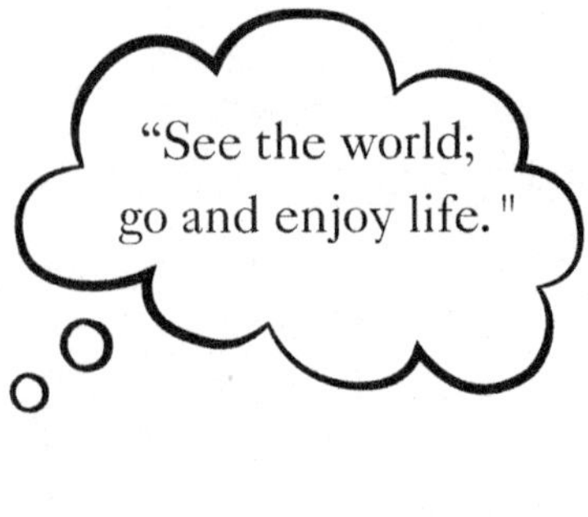

You were right, Mum.

And so, I resigned at ICI, which wasn't an easy task, and it came as a shock to some of my colleagues. They would say,

"You're leaving ICI?"

"What about your pension? Your share options? The job security?"

"This is a job for life; you don't just walk away from ICI."

"You'll never get a better job than this..."

And honestly? They were all correct. ICI was a great company. It had looked after me. But sometimes, life isn't about playing it safe. Sometimes, it's about following that voice inside you.

And for me it was time to wave goodbye.

New Zealand here I come.

"The lessons that shape us often
come disguised as breakdowns.
Whether it's a failed exam,
a seized gearbox, or a life detour,
each failure leaves behind
a blueprint
for
resilience and reliability;
if only we choose to study it."

Chapter 3

A Lightbulb Moment

A Lightbulb Moment

"Optimism is the faith that leads to achievement. Nothing can be done without hope and confidence."
Helen Keller

Landing in New Zealand marked the start of a brand-new chapter, not just in geography, but in mindset. I had left behind the security and familiarity of ICI to chase something different: growth, adventure, and the kind of challenge that wakes you up in the morning with purpose.

What I didn't expect was how quickly I'd be tested, both professionally and personally.

In this chapter, I share one of the most confronting experiences of my career. What began as a routine day on site quickly turned into a life-altering event, reminding me that safety, communication, and accountability are not just policies; they are lifelines. The memory of what happened still sits with me, as do the emotions, shock, guilt, frustration, and ultimately, resolve.

It was this incident that set me on a new path.

I discovered the value of structured problem-solving and how the right tools, such as the Apollo Root Cause Analysis method, can help organisations shift from blame to understanding. And also, being a reliability engineer isn't just about fixing machines; it's about protecting people. And it's in moments like these, when things don't go to plan, that the real lessons begin.

A LEAP INTO THE UNKNOWN

My girlfriend, Sharon, and I, who had recently graduated as a midwife, agreed to take the plunge and try life out in New Zealand. It was one of those exciting, slightly scary decisions you make when you're young and chasing a dream. So, after a farewell party with friends and family, we packed a rucksack each and headed off to Manchester Airport, with an unknown future ahead of us.

Leaving friends and family, without a doubt, was the toughest part of the decision. But it was still the right decision.

Knowing I was leaving my dad and sister behind, especially after we had lost Mum, was difficult. But we kept telling ourselves: we are only going to be a 24-hour flight away. We could talk on the phone (we didn't have Zoom back then!), they could come and visit, and we'd always stay connected. Life will still be good.

When we landed in Auckland with no jobs lined up for when we reached New Zealand. We didn't have much planning. Apart from that, the first few nights were booked in a youth hostel in Auckland, and then it was time to travel.

We bought a map of New Zealand and started planning the trip in those first few days. I had visited New Zealand on a previous holiday and fell in love with the country. I always had a desire to return and spend more time here, and here I was, actually doing it.

For the first time since I turned 16 years old, I felt freedom. I had no job to rush to, I had no income, just living off savings and leaning into the adventure. It felt amazing to be free! A road trip and a whole new chapter of life lay ahead. We didn't know exactly where the road would take us, but we were ready for it, all in, hearts open, and spirits high.

After several unforgettable months of amazing travel and soaking up everything New Zealand had to offer, we came to the not-so-romantic realisation. As much as we loved the freedom and spontaneity of our travels, it was time to face reality. We decided to start looking for work opportunities, as the savings were not going to last forever.

At that point, I wasn't sure if I wanted to have a career change. Sharon and I were both open to something new, we both looked at other options away from what we had been trained in, even if it meant stepping way outside our comfort zones. We threw around some ideas, most of which were random. We even considered something called 'share milking' which involves managing a dairy farm on behalf of the owner, usually providing the labour, equipment and expertise in exchange for a share of the milk income.

It seemed like a smart move, especially with Sharon's farming background. She grew up on a farm in Ireland, after all. But soon after, I found out she was scared of cows after being knocked over by one when she was younger! That put an abrupt end to our brief cow-farming dreams. Never mind, the thought was nice while it lasted.

To be honest, I wasn't sure getting up at 3am to milk the cows was right for me. I knew deep down that my passion for reliability was still there. I'd worked hard to build that knowledge; I knew I could make a difference, and if given the opportunity, I could bring real value to a company. So, I was back to reading the New Zealand Herald newspaper.

One morning, while flicking through the 'Engineering Vacancies' section, I spotted a position of 'Reliability Engineer' with a company called the Mars Corporation. The location of the role was at a pet food factory called 'Lucky Petfoods' in a town called Wanganui (pronounced Phonga-nui), as I soon learnt, Whangarei was pronounced Ph-ongaray, Whakatane was Ph-ockatane, Whakapapa was

Phokapapa – Well... let's just say I had to get comfortable replacing 'Wh' with a 'Ph'!

At that point, we were still living in Auckland. Lucky Petfood kindly offered to fly me down to Wanganui on a small aeroplane, and they would then collect me from Wanganui and drive me to the site.

I thought, "Wow, that's pretty generous."

I boarded the flight at Auckland airport and remember thinking how small the aircraft was. I had been on a small Cessna before for a pleasure trip in Las Vegas and remember saying back then I wouldn't fly propeller planes again. I couldn't help myself. My brain went straight into Reliability Engineer mode. One single engine on the front always made me think of those 'single points of failure' I had dealt with at ICI. And I couldn't stop thinking: what if the aircraft engineer had installed second-hand bearings because his manager told him to?

Anyway, I just crossed my fingers and hoped that whoever maintained this little bird believed in preventative maintenance as much as I did. So, there I was mid-journey to Wanganui. The aircraft was cosy, to say the least, with six people on board, the pilot, copilot and yes, a stewardess too. We had an uneventful flight, and I observed some amazing New Zealand scenery.

THE ONE-MAN AIRPORT

Eventually, we landed safely at Wanganui airport. When I looked out the window, I genuinely chuckled. I remember thinking how small this airport was! I saw the young guy, an airport worker, out on the tarmac, waving the aircraft into position with his tennis bats. Once we stopped, he placed chocks under the aircraft's wheels, plugged the aircraft in, then he got the steps to the aircraft. As we stepped off the aircraft, he cheerfully asked for everyone’s hand luggage. At which point, I offered to carry mine, but he insisted on putting them on a trolley.

Then off he went, he wheeled the trolley full of our bags across to the small, unassuming airport building. The five other passengers and I were quietly entertained, exchanging smiles among ourselves while watching the airport worker work. He was literally doing everything at this airport. In fact, we didn’t see anyone else working there at all.

As we stood around, he then disappeared behind a wall and started a small conveyor.

Slowly, through a hole in the wall, the bags began to appear one by one. The old conveyor made so much noise; it sounded like it was about to fall apart at any moment. Honestly, it looked like it was in desperate need of some maintenance.

The passengers and I couldn't help but laugh as we could easily have carried our hand luggage, meaning this would've been one less task for the overworked airport worker. We started joking that maybe he owned the airport and took great pride in ensuring everything was done correctly.

However, the funniest bit was still to come.

As I looked around for my 'driver' who was supposed to collect me from Lucky Petfoods, the airport owner moved behind a desk (or 'disk' as they pronounce it here in New Zealand), literally less than two meters away from where I was standing.

He announced from the Tannoy, "Would passenger Tyne, who recently arrived on flight 123 from Auckland airport, please report to the reception desk?" The announcement echoed around the nearly empty airport building on the loudspeakers. I mean, no other flights had arrived in the last hour, and there were only about five people in the building at this stage; it's not like anyone was going to miss that!

Trying not to laugh too hard, I approached the desk and said, "Yes, I'm Tyne, recently arrived from Auckland."

He smiled and said he had a message for me. Unfortunately, Lucky Petfoods were unable to collect me but had arranged for a hire car which I could use to drive to the factory.

This wasn't a problem, I thought. I mean, how hard could it be to pick up a hire car from this tiny airport?

I asked him, "Where can I collect the hire car from?"

The airport owner (by now, I was sure he was the owner) pointed casually across the room to a small desk with a small sign with rental car hire on it and behind it hung a long, flowing, old curtain. "There," he said simply, giving a slight nod toward the desk, as if it were the most obvious thing. Anyway, I thanked him and headed to the desk.

As I approached the desk, I saw a small bell with a sign next to it that said: "Ring for Attention". So, I followed the instructions and I gave the bell a gentle tap. And just like a magician appearing on cue, the curtain behind the desk suddenly opened, and out stepped, yes, you guessed it; the same airport owner! I stood there blinking; I couldn't believe it. I mean, was this real? Was this guy a clone?

Were there five versions of him secretly wandering around the airport doing these airport duties? This was getting crazy, but then get this, he leaned forward and asked, "Can I help you?"

That was it; I just lost it. I just broke down in laughter, wiping my tears away. Through my chuckles, I managed to say, "You just sent me over here, from that desk over there!"

but he was deadly serious, never cracked a smile. It was starting to feel like I was on some hilarious hidden camera show! Still giggling, I took a deep breath and tried to focus as he passed me a rental form to sign and asked me for my driver's licence. I patted my pockets, checked my bag, and then realised I had no driving licence on me. I had left it back at my accommodation in Auckland! I had no need to bring it as I was supposed to be collected straight from the airport, but now my plans had unexpectedly changed.

I explained my little dilemma to the airport owner, who, by now, was also the owner of the hire car business.

He simply said, "Can you drive?"

I said, "Of course I can!"

Without a second thought, he reached under the desk, pulled out a set of car keys, and handed them to me, just like that. He told me that the hired car was already parked outside, was ready and waiting for me to collect. He informed me it had been freshly delivered from the local Holden Dealer in town and had less than 50km on the clock. I couldn't believe I was able to take the keys to what turned out to be an awesome 5.7 litre Holden Commodore.

What a machine!

I double-checked and then double-checked again, as I asked, “Are you sure I can take the car without you seeing my driving licence?”.

I imagined trying to take a hire car in the UK without showing a driving licence, but this would never happen. But here in New Zealand, this place is laid back and life is chilled.

The airport owner, or let’s just say the hire car business owner, smiled, gave a little shrug, and said the words that perfectly captured the spirit of the place:

"She'll be right, mate”.

it’s a phrase often associated with Australia, but also used in New Zealand, and is an expression of optimism and a belief that things will eventually work out. I told him I could drive, and he trusted me, just like that. No fuss. He also trusted that I would return the car. Yes, as you can see, this place was different.

I got into my shiny new Commodore, fired up that beautiful engine and headed across town to the ‘Lucky Petfoods’ company in Wanganui.

NOT QUITE MY SCENE

I was met at reception by a friendly manager who shook my hand and led me down a hallway into a room for the interview. Everything started off pretty standard, no surprises. We went through all the usual questions:

Where do you see yourself in five years?
What are your strengths?
What are your weaknesses?
Why should we hire you?

You know the type. I answered as best as I could, trying to sound confident but not cocky. We spent a considerable amount of time discussing reliability in detail, and I asked a few questions about the role, the company, and the facility itself. For a moment, I was going to ask the manager about the airport and if he knew the owner, but I didn't, because honestly, it was such a small town, I was certain he knew him. Everyone probably knew everyone. Best to stay focused. After the interview, the manager stood up, clapped his hands together, and said, "Right then, let's go take a look around the plant."

I was actually pretty excited. I had never been in a pet food company before, so I was looking forward to the tour. I had imagined seeing big, shiny machines and workers bustling around, but it wasn't long before I found myself retching from the awful smell.

It was like getting punched in the nose by a rotting seafood market. I tried to act casual, breathing through my mouth. As we moved through the plant, he pointed out large fish heads and chicken feet being put through a large, dangerous-looking grinding machine, which turned them into some kind of paste.

I tried to keep a neutral face, but honestly, inside, I was screaming. And just when I thought it couldn't get any worse, we arrived at the blood tank. Now, I didn't exactly tell anyone that I'm a bit faint-hearted around blood (okay, a lot faint-hearted). In my mind, I tried to stay calm by imagining myself sitting on a beach in the sun. But then, mid-mental beach vacation, I heard the Manager casually explain, "And the blood gets sent around from vessel A into B...". I made the mistake of looking.

That's when I spotted a technician dressed head-to-toe in white overalls and white Wellington boots, frantically trying to stop a leak on a Wilden double diaphragm pump. With every pulse of air, blood was squirting out of the leaking gasket, splashing all over his white overalls. It looked like a full-blown murder scene. I had seen enough, or so I thought. But nope, there was more.

Next, I was taken to an area of the plant classified as 'Top Secret'. I was told I was about to look at the latest innovation in technology.

Something that was 'apparently' the world's first, which would take the pet food industry by storm. The anticipation was killing me. What could it be? What was behind this door that only a few people had seen before me?

The heavy door creaked open dramatically, and there in front of me was the first-ever cat food pouch filling machine in the world, filling pouches with, yes, you guessed it, cat food. The packaging had writing all over it, the language of which was either Korean or Japanese; I wasn't sure, and apparently, this was the market where the pouches were being sold. My host, practically buzzing with excitement, turned to me and said, “Well, what do you think?”

I tried hard to look impressed, but having never owned a cat or purchased cat food before, I was struggling to match his level of enthusiasm.

“We can’t afford for this to break down, it’s our future, and this needs to be reliable”, he told me.

I nodded seriously, but I couldn’t help but remember that I actually had bought cat food before. Yes, I know, you read it right earlier, I don’t have a cat. It was a time when I accidentally bought cat food. It happened years ago, during a trip to France. I’d picked up a small, fancy-looking tin at a supermarket, thinking it was some kind of gourmet pâté, for which I had big plans; I was going to use it with my cheese, crackers and wine that evening. But when I finally sat down to eat, the first bite didn't taste nice. Well, the small picture of a cat on the tin should've given it away really... Anyway, my visit to the plant came to an end, and I shook hands with the team, and asked politely, "When might I expect to hear back about the job?".

One of them smiled and replied, "Pretty soon, but we do have a few more candidates to interview first."

As I walked out, I remember thinking, I hope they aren't scared of blood and guts like I am. I made my way back to Wanganui (which, by the way, is pronounced 'Phonganui') in my top-of-the-range fast 5.7 litre Holden Commodore. As I pulled up to the small airport, I wondered if the airport owner would be there to greet me at the reception again. Sure enough, there he was. I handed him the car keys and grinned.

"So," I asked, "Will you be flying me back to Auckland this fine evening?"

He apologised, shook his head and said, "Flying the aircraft is about the only job I don't do here at the airport," he said, "but everything else, you can rely on me!"

And to be fair, he wasn't wrong. The guy ran a tight ship.

Funny enough, before my return flight to Auckland had landed, I had already made my decision to turn down the lucky pet food role if it was offered to me. Sure, the trip had its charm, but something didn't sit right. Back in the UK, I had worked on some big equipment at ICI. That factory I'd just toured? It reminded me of a Meccano set in comparison. In fact, I remember building some larger Meccano toys as a child. So, the job just didn't spark that excitement I was looking for.

Yes, I needed to keep looking. But I wasn't in any rush; I was enjoying this freedom, and the open road was still calling for travel and adventure. Something better would turn up, I could feel it. Until then, why not enjoy the ride?

The following morning, I got a call from the agency that had arranged my interview in Wanganui.

"Good news!" the agent said brightly. "They've offered you the role of Site Reliability Engineer!"

I paused for a moment, unsure of how to respond. Part of me was surprised. Really? They picked me?

I remember thinking that the other candidates had probably declined the interview, maybe they had heard about the blood and guts, or maybe there were no other candidates to begin with?

Trying to keep things polite and professional, I had to tell the agent straight away that I would not be accepting the role, that the factory wasn't to my liking and thanked him for the opportunity. I hung up feeling a bit uncertain, but also relieved. I knew I'd made the right decision. Something better would come along.

A VIEW WORTH THE MOVE

A few days later, I was reading the New Zealand Herald and as I opened the job section there it was. A site Reliability Engineer position on offer in a place called Kapuni at a Shell Oil facility. Now this sounded interesting. No blood and guts with this role, just technical and industrial work. That was more my scene.

I applied online, and a few days later, I got a call for an interview. It was near a city called New Plymouth that advertised itself as the surf capital and the only place in New Zealand where you could surf and ski in one day.

"Surf and ski in one place?" I chuckled. "Now that's impressive."

Now the skiing was appealing, but the surfing? Not so much. My knowledge of sharks in the oceans was definitely going to keep me out of the water. I was allowed to watch 'Jaws' as a youngster. I still blame my parents, because it instilled a fear in me that is still with me to this day.

Every time I step into the sea for a paddle, I hear 'dum dum...dum. 'Dum dum. Dumdumdumdumdumdum.......... terrifying soundtrack of the Jaws music. Even writing this down makes me get a cold shiver.

Anyway, I agreed to attend the interview in New Plymouth. It felt like a solid next step. While I was sorting that out, Sharon also rang the Taranaki Base Hospital and enquired about any open midwife positions. To our surprise, they said they would like to meet her. We both had possible opportunities here. The Oil and Gas opportunity sounded more aligned to the role I had been working in with ICI back in the UK, engineering, machinery, and reliability. No animal parts, blood and guts. This felt more like my world.

So, we packed our bags and headed on the road from Auckland down to New Plymouth. We had booked a few nights of accommodation to give us a chance to explore the area. New Plymouth is in a region called Taranaki or ‘The Naki’ as it is known to the locals. We followed the winding road down State Highway 3, through some strange-sounding locations like ‘Pio Pio’. And then came ‘The Awakino Gorge’. The road twisted and turned, thick forests lining each side. I slowed the car a little and glanced around. It really looked like we had stepped into the film set of Jurassic Park, and any minute we expected a Tyrannosaurus Rex to appear from the trees at the side of the road.

The scenery and road trip were spectacular. Then we were greeted with a view like no other, and I will never forget the first time I set eyes on her.

A perfect cone, her snow-capped peak piercing the clear blue sky, surrounded by a delicate ring of white clouds, there she was: Mount Taranaki in all her glory, looking at us from across the ocean. What a view.

Honestly, it was breathtaking. The way the mountain rose up so gracefully from the land was very similar in shape to Mount Fuji in Japan. I had only seen it in pictures at school, but the shape was so similar. When I used to draw volcanoes in art class at junior school, this was the volcano I was drawing and painting. A dormant volcano right in the middle of the Naki!

It holds deep cultural meaning, too. It was named after Rua Taranaki, the first ancestor of the iwi (tribe) called Taranaki. Then, along came Captain Cook, who named it Mount Egmont on 11th January 1770 after John Percival, 2nd Earl of Egmont, who had supported the oceanic search for Terra Australis Incognita. Cook described Taranaki as 'of a prodigious height and its top covered with everlasting snow'. He was spot on.

This was a sight to behold and one that I will always cherish.

RELIABILITY IN THE LAND OF THE LONG WHITE CLOUD

The interview in New Plymouth was scheduled for the following day. Unfortunately, so was the bad weather. The weather had taken a turn for the worse. The sky had turned a dark grey early in the morning, and by the time we were getting ready, rain had already started falling, big, heavy drops that looked like they had plans to stay. I was told the interview would only take an hour, as I already had a phone interview. As we pulled into the offices in New Plymouth, the plan was for Sharon to wait for me in the car.

So, I turned to her and said, "Shouldn't be too long," and then left.

What was supposed to be a one-hour formality turned into a full technical session, lots of back and forth about machinery, maintenance schedules, reliability framework; it was actually a great discussion. But I kept glancing at the clock and then at the window. Outside, the weather had taken a dramatic turn. It was raining heavily, with intermittent hailstones, and the sky had turned very dark. Before long, the thunder and lightning started to crash around the building. I remembered I had left Sharon in the car parked outside and wondered how she was coping because not only was she in the middle of a full-on thunderstorm, she also had a deep fear of lightning.

I had only discovered this fear a few months earlier, quite by accident, while we were on our tour around New Zealand. We had been staying in Queenstown on the South Island and had taken a day trip to Milford Sound. It was given the name Milford in 1823 by a sealer named John Grono, who named it after Milford Haven, his birthplace in Wales. It is also one of the wettest places in New Zealand.

So, no surprise that it was raining on the day of our visit.

Regardless, I was excited to see Mitre Peak, one of New Zealand's most iconic and spectacular sights, rising straight out of the water like something from a postcard.

The road trip was around four hours long, and when we finally arrived in Milford, we parked up carefully as the weather was pretty awful. We set off across the car park to the ticket office, when, out of nowhere and without warning, a massive crack of lightning appeared in the sky and, in a split second, struck the surface of the sound.

Before I had a chance to say anything, Sharon was already back inside the car, a quivering wreck. She said she wasn't going on a boat in this weather and that she had a fear of lightning.

Considering my shark phobia and Sharon's fear of lightning, we knew our journey down under would be an adventure!

While sitting in a meeting room with thunder rumbling and lightning flashing outside, all I could think about was poor Sharon in that parked car.

So, as the interview finally came to an end, I was offered the role. What a relief! It was my second interview, and it was deeper than the first. They really dug into my knowledge of reliability. My hands-on experience with reliability swung it in my favour!

When I left the building and headed for the car in the torrential rain and lightning, I was soaking wet, my heart sinking a little with worry just knowing Sharon would be quivering in the car. I had only planned to be an hour, maybe a little more. But the whole thing had stretched into at least two hours. I just knew Sharon would be waiting nervously in the car. She hated storms, and I felt awful for leaving her in that situation.

I got to the car, and Sharon had gone. My heart skipped a beat. I checked the boot of the car just in case she had climbed in there to escape the thunder, but nothing. I was worried. Where was she? I looked around frantically, the rain blurring my vision, when I suddenly spotted her waving at me from a nearby sports bar window... It turns out that two kind-hearted Kiwi guys had seen her quivering in the car. They checked to see if she was okay, realising she wasn't.

She explained she was waiting for me to return. They suggested taking shelter in the local bar...Being an Irish girl, she didn't need to be asked twice, and there she was, safely drinking a beer with two new Kiwi friends - her knights in shining armour. I thanked them sincerely, and then we headed back to our accommodation.

The reliability role turned out to be a fantastic opportunity.

It was based at a remote site called Kapuni, approximately. 60km from New Plymouth. There was just one final step, I needed to meet with the client 'Shell Todd Oil Services' and if they were happy with me, then I had got the job. That meeting was arranged, and everything clicked into place. They gave the green light.

At the same time, things were lining up beautifully for Sharon as well. She had also been offered a midwifery role at the Taranaki base hospital. Our future in New Zealand was being laid. It felt like the pieces of our new life were falling perfectly into place. We arranged for some rental property viewings and started to plan our future here, in the shadow of Mount Taranaki in the land of the long white cloud. It felt right.

Back during the interview, I had been told the job involved working fourteen-hour days, which I remember thinking, "Wow, that's excessive", but we did get Fridays off.

Still, I wasn't entirely sure how I'd manage such long days. Later, when my contract landed, I realised I had totally misheard the description and in fact the role was four ten-hour days – not fourteen-hour days.

With a kiwi accent, the 'ten' was pronounced 'tin' and I had confused it for 'fourteen'. This made me smile, but I also breathed a sigh of relief.

"Well, that's much more manageable," I thought.

The role involved initially being picked up by my manager and driving to the site, which was about 60 km away. Once we arrived at the site, I conducted some inductions and was introduced to several of the site technicians I'd be working with. There was Barry, Scooter, Brett, Kevin, the store manager and Ian 'sticky' McNab, the condition monitoring engineer.

I was brought on as the site Reliability Engineer and worked alongside the Process Engineer, Mechanical Engineer, Electrical Engineer and Integrity Engineer. My role was to implement across the site the concept of reliability and to ensure the equipment worked smoothly, consistently, and didn't break down unexpectedly.

FROM END OF LIFE TO NEW BEGINNINGS

It turned out that the facility had been experiencing a period of decline for several years. The main reason was due to diminishing 'condensate'.

As a result, the maintenance budgets had been cut, and the Operating Expenditure (Opex) spend had not been invested in maintenance. Condensate is basically a mixture of gas and oil that is recovered from underground reservoirs. The site then separated both the oil and gas. The oil was pumped to the local port in New Plymouth to be sent for processing at the Whangarei refinery in New Zealand, and the gas was either transported from the site by train or sent next door to be entered into the nation's gas supply managed by the National Gas Corporation of New Zealand. It was a complex operation, and everything had to work in sync.

Now, here's where it gets interesting and a bit classic New Zealand. They had experienced an earthquake that opened another possible twenty-year supply of condensate that had previously been unknown. So, the facility, which had been running down on its maintenance program and was considered an end-of-life asset, suddenly had a future; another 20-25 years of production demand was predicted.

That changed everything. So, in terms of reliability, the reliability team had a huge task ahead.

We were no longer maintaining a dying asset; we were being asked to breathe new life into it. Maintaining an end-of-life (EOL) asset is a delicate but crucial part of any reliability strategy. Even though the asset is near the end of its design life or is due for replacement, it still plays a critical part in the operation right now. It still has to run safely, day in and day out.

Until end-of-life assets are removed or replaced, they deserve attention, discipline, and care to protect the plant, people, and the business.

From a reliability point of view, this meant we had to shift our strategy. We had to build a proper reliability plan, prioritising critical systems, focusing on preventative maintenance, bringing in condition monitoring tools, and above all, getting the correct data to make smart decisions. It wasn't going to be easy, but now we had a reason to invest the time, the energy, and the budget.

One of the important aspects of any reliability journey is ensuring we have the right culture in place. You can have all the tools, plans, and systems in the world, but if the people aren't on board, it's not going to work.

It didn't take me long to acknowledge that we had some serious challenges in that area. There were clear signs that the team wasn't exactly motivated.

Initially, I could not understand why people were demotivated and, to some degree, not concerned that equipment was failing. It puzzled me until I understood the backstory.

The maintenance staff had previously been Shell employees, but the maintenance contract was taken on by Transfield Worley. As a result, the Shell staff were now contractors and doing the same work while earning less money. Some had taken big pay cuts. No wonder morale had taken a hit.

So, this was going to be a tough gig. So here I was, trying to lead a reliability program at a facility running on end-of-life equipment that had been under-maintained for the last five years... and with a maintenance team that was demotivated following the maintenance contract handover.

I do enjoy a challenge, but I won't lie, I did wonder for a moment if that Pet Food Reliability Engineer position in Wanganui was still open.

The first week onsite was all about getting to know people, walking around, and trying to understand how things worked. The good thing is that the views from this facility were overlooking Mount Taranaki. This remains one of the most scenic locations I have ever worked.

"How lucky am I?" I thought more than once.

THE ROOT CAUSE REFLECTION

I was asked to attend some Root Cause Analysis (RCA) training in New Plymouth. It was called Apollo RCA training. I remember telling the site manager Allan that I had performed RCAs in my previous role with ICI and used 5 Whys and Ishikawa (the fishbone diagram). Although I wasn't a massive fan of the techniques and had some frustrations with them, I was told the site was going to use Apollo and insisted that I attend.

When it comes to solving problems, especially in complex maintenance issues, it's essential to choose the right tools.

While I did find Ishikawa, an excellent brainstorming tool, it did not, in my view, identify root causes or effective solutions, and my reasons for finding it frustrating are:

1. Too Generic or Overused Categories
Fishbone diagrams traditionally use standard categories like Methods, Machines, Materials, Manpower, Measurement, and Environment (the 6Ms). These can feel forced or irrelevant in certain contexts, which can make the exercise feel like box-ticking rather than real problem-solving.

2. Brainstorming Without Depth
People sometimes treat fishbone diagrams as a quick brainstorming tool and stop at surface-level causes.

That results in vague entries like “lack of training” or “poor communication,” without digging deeper into the "why" behind those issues.

3. Too Much or Too Little Input

- Too much input: If a large group contributes all at once, it can quickly get cluttered and chaotic.
- Too little input: If the right people aren’t involved, or if people don’t speak up, it ends up shallow or incomplete.

4. No Prioritisation or Follow-Through

Fishbone diagrams can turn into a “wall of causes” with no clear direction on what to do next. Without tools like Pareto analysis, 5 Whys, or data to validate the causes, it’s hard to know what to focus on.

5. It's Not Always Visual or Collaborative Enough

When done with sticky notes on a wall, it can be interactive and engaging. However, when it's just a static diagram in a report or drawn by one person in isolation, it loses impact and feels disconnected from the team's insight.

6. Not Suited for Complex or Systemic Issues

Fishbone diagrams are neat and structured, and they're particularly effective when dealing with technical issues or process-related problems that have clear cause-and-effect relationships, where the causes are easy to identify. However, once you begin addressing complex or multilayered problems, such as cultural issues, long-term maintenance failures, or people-related challenges, these diagrams can fall short of providing a comprehensive solution. Fishbone diagrams can oversimplify the situation.

The 5 Whys, on the other hand, was too linear and based on the 'Ask Why Five Times' approach, where the root cause would magically appear at the end of the cause path. It is a good starting point and can be done quickly at the coal face or down on the production line, but it's not always the best choice for more complex, recurring or systemic issues. So yes, 5 Whys is a helpful tool. But, just remember, it's not a one-size-fits-all solution. Use it wisely and know when to switch to deeper problem-solving methods when the situation calls for it.

Now, here are a few more reasons for being cautious when using 5 Whys:

1. Over-Simplification of Complex Problems: 5 Whys assumes there's a single linear cause-and-effect path, but real-world problems often have multiple contributing factors. By chasing just one thread, you can miss the systemic or interacting causes.

2. Lack of Data or Evidence: If the team relies solely on opinions or assumptions (rather than data or evidence), you risk chasing the wrong root cause.

This can lead to wasted effort on fixes that don't solve the actual problem.

3. Subjectivity and Inconsistency: There's no strict structure, which means outcomes can vary wildly depending on who's in the room. Different people asking the exact 5 Whys can arrive at different causes, depending on:
   - Their perspective
   - Their biases
   - What they think is "reasonable" to ask next

4. Stops at Symptoms or Blame: Some teams stop too early, after 2 or 3 whys, or land on vague conclusions like "operator error" or "poor training." These are symptoms, not root causes. Worse, they can promote blame rather than improvement.

5. No Built-in Validation or Follow-Up: The 5 Whys doesn't include steps to:
   - Confirm if the identified cause is valid
   - Test countermeasures
   - Track effectiveness

It really needs to be paired with other tools (like PDCA, data analysis, or A3 thinking) to close the loop.

6. Not Well-Documented: The simplicity of the method means that people often do it informally or fail to write it down correctly.

That can lead to:

- Poor communication
- Loss of learning
- Inability to audit or improve the process

7. Ignores Systemic or Organisational Issues: If the root cause involves cultural, structural, or leadership issues, the 5 Whys process may gloss over them or stop short, because it's hard or uncomfortable to ask "why" about those topics.

So, based on my previous RCA frustrations with previous root cause analysis (RCA) attempts, I agreed to go to the 'Apollo RCA' training course. It was being held in New Plymouth, and I promised myself I'd go in with an open mind. It is a new learning experience, and that is an essential element of a reliability journey. It's vital to stay educated and learn new techniques and initiatives to keep pace with the rapidly evolving world of reliability, with the latest tools, techniques, and approaches emerging all the time.

If you are not learning, you are falling behind. The more you know, the sharper your thinking becomes. You start recognising patterns faster, understanding root causes more clearly, and asking much better questions. It's like building a mental toolbox; you may not need every tool all the time, but when the right problem comes along, you're ready.

THE ROOT CAUSE REVOLUTION

So here it was, day one of the Apollo RCA course, it was a public training course with two experienced trainers running the show, Jason and Nerida from ARMS reliability, all the way from Australia. From the very beginning, the course started to challenge some of the ways I had been taught about RCA. It really made me pause and reflect on how I had previously performed investigations in the past. And honestly? It was refreshing, it made sense.

The Apollo process had structure, logic, and clarity. I could see how it offered a better framework for tackling problems, especially the tricky, recurring ones.

We were introduced to the book written by the founder of Apollo Root Cause Analysis Methodology - Mr Dean Gano. Its title was 'A New Way of Thinking,' and that is precisely what it was, a new way of thinking, a different mindset, a new lens for seeing and solving problems.

Mr Gano was a mechanical engineer and started his fascination with problem-solving by working on the Three Mile Island incident in the United States back in 1979. Mr Gano began writing articles for technical magazines in the USA, generating considerable interest with his approach. His ideas started gaining attention, and before long, his method began to take off.

That was the birthplace of the Apollo RCA methodology.

<u>The methodology is based on four key steps</u>:

1 Define the Problem
2 Build the Cause-and-Effect Chart
3 Identify Solutions
4 Implement Solutions

One thing that really stood out to me in the Apollo RCA training was their use of the phrase "caused by" when linking causes together. I actually mentioned this phrase back in Chapter 2, and since then, it has become second nature for me to use it. Looking back, I honestly believe this training course quite possibly changed my career path.

Years before this, and during the RCA training with ICI, I was introduced to the Fishbone and 5 Whys techniques. Like I mentioned earlier, those tools were helpful to an extent, but nobody had taught me the principles of cause and effect. And this was where the real lightbulb moment happened for me. I actually felt it, the shift in my thinking.

<u>The four principles of cause and effect are</u>:

1 Cause and Effect are the Same Thing
2 Each Effect has at least two Causes in the form of Actions and Conditions

3 Causes and Effects are part of an Infinite Continuum of Causes
4 An Effect only exists if its Causes exist in the same time and frame

Principle number 2 was the lightbulb moment. It talks about the difference between actions and conditions. Actions are momentary, and conditions exist over time. Let me break this down a bit.

Actions are the things people do in a moment, like pressing a button, making a decision, or overlooking a check. Actions can also be other activities that happen in a moment that are not human-related. Conditions, on the other hand, are the background factors, things that build up over time, such as poor training, unclear procedures, or a culture that discourages speaking up.

Here's the powerful bit: If you only focus on actions, you are starting to proportion blame; if you ignore conditions, then the chances are this problem will recur. Boom! That was the real aha! Moment for me.

It hit me hard because I realised how true this was in my own experience. “If you only focus on actions, you are starting to proportion blame...”, I repeated in my head.

A lot of investigations I were involved in during my early

career at ICI involved just looking at actions. And honestly, we focused on actions because they are easy. It's easy to blame someone rather than examining the underlying causes of a problem.

"Why did you stop the pump?"
"Why did you not shut the valve?"
"Why did you close the door?"
"Why did you...?" The list goes on...

It was all about actions. That's just how things were done. Very rarely did we stop to talk about conditions, the background issues or system weaknesses that might've led to the problem. Even going back to my first RCA on 3J24, I remember the finger-pointing clearly. People were quick to blame the mechanical seal manufacturer, as if the problem was just a bad part.

Then there was the issue with the compactor gearbox — maintenance got the blame for not lubricating it properly. It was a classic blame culture. Operations always blamed maintenance, and maintenance always blamed operations. That's how it was. On the other hand, if you can change, control or mitigate a condition, you are far better placed to prevent the problem from recurring.

Back at ICI, and before I moved into a reliability role, I was overseeing a project inside the sand filter building.

Part of the job involved installing a platform at height, between the two sand filters, to enable easier access. Every day, towards the end of the day, I would ensure all the power tools were isolated and the area was tidy, ready for the start of the following day.

Putting this in the context of principle 2, that was the action of the visible part. But behind that action were the conditions that influenced it: clear expectations, good planning, and a strong focus on safety.

At the time, the sand filter building was shut down and closed to everyone except the project team. No equipment was running, so it was quiet. One day, while I was working, I suddenly heard the large sliding door open. Curious, I looked over the scaffolding and saw a site electrician walking over to the sand filters. He was doing his weekly PH testing round.

I called down to him and said, “Hey, the filters are empty, and nothing is running. The testing isn’t required.” He nodded, but didn’t say much, so I turned around and continued with my task.

A few moments later, I heard the electrician climbing the vertical ladder between the two filters. This immediately alarmed me, because the vertical ladder had a ‘No Entry’ sign on it. It was not safe to use, as the exit platform at the top had been removed for the project.

I quickly turned to call out another warning, but before I could, I witnessed the electrician lose his footing. In one hand, he was carrying a small toolbox with his test equipment, and he was holding the ladder with the other. When his foot reached the rungs of the ladder that had a clear 'No Entry' sign, he lost three points of contact and fell backwards. His safety helmet fell off during the fall, and he hit his head hard on a welded lifting eye attached to the tank right behind him. It was a terrible moment to witness. I immediately climbed down the scaffolding ladder to rush to his aid.

When I reached him, I saw he was already bleeding from the nose and ears. He was conscious but looked confused and dazed. I knelt down and I told him to stay there while I got help. I ran to call the site first aider, and since we were near the gatehouse, we also called an ambulance immediately. I was in shock. I just stood there for a moment, trying to take it all in. My heart was racing.

I kept thinking, "How did this happen?"

He must not have heard me shout at him that no testing was required. I should have shouted louder. Then another thought hit me: "How did he get into the building? It was closed to everyone other than project personnel!"

I just kept thinking over and over, "Why? Why? Why?"

Later that day, the news came back from the hospital that the individual had suffered a fracture to his skull and would be away from work for some time. Hearing that made my stomach drop. I felt awful.

Then came the investigation into the incident. It started almost immediately. I was interviewed and questioned several times. I tried to stay calm and give honest answers, but inside, I was still shaken up.

The one question I clearly remember was "Who put the safety sign across the vertical ladder?"

I replied honestly, "That was me. I placed it there to prevent people from climbing the ladder."

What they said next really shocked me. They told me, "Well, if you hadn't put that sign there, maybe he wouldn't have fallen."

For a second, I didn't know what to say. I felt I was being blamed for this accident. It didn't make sense to me.

Why was nobody asking the critical questions?
Why was he carrying a toolbox up a ladder?
Why did he ignore the no-entry sign?
How did he get access to the building?

But no one seemed to be asking any of that. Instead, the focus was on me, on the sign. They were looking for someone to blame. A scapegoat. And in that moment, it felt like I was the easy target. But deep down, I knew I had done the right thing, and I was not prepared to accept blame for something I didn't cause.

Fortunately, I was able to produce the permit to work for the project. It clearly identified the need for a safety sign on the vertical ladder to stop anyone from climbing the ladder during construction work. It was right there, in black and white. I had put the sign on the ladder because it had been issued as a requirement on the project permit. I had followed the safety rules that were officially given.

That sign was there to protect people, not harm them.

The individual in question eventually returned to work on light duties. We were all relieved to see him back. He wasn't quite the same, but he was making progress, and we hoped he'd fully recover over time. That's why it came as such a shock when we heard that, several months later, he had unexpectedly passed away in his sleep. It hit me hard. I've never forgotten him, that incident or the investigation that followed. It stays with you. You can't help but replay things in your mind, wondering if anything could have been done differently. One thing I've learned from that experience is the importance of focusing on solutions, not blame.

That's why I really connected with the Apollo RCA method. It's designed to identify practical solutions by looking at all the contributing factors. It does not seek blame!

I love the quote by John F Kennedy, the 35th President of the United States. He said,

"Things do not happen. Things are made to happen."

He used those words to emphasise the importance of action, planning and leadership. It is also an excellent mindset for the reliability journey. Success isn't accidental; it's intentional.

So, after completing my Apollo RCA training, I returned to my site Reliability Engineer role at Kapuni. On my first day back, the Site Manager met me and asked, "How was the training?"

I was very enthusiastic and eager to start using the approach to address some of the reliability and production issues the plant was experiencing. I mentioned how the method works; identifying actions and condition-based causes to come up with effective long-term solutions. I told him I was ready to start applying this new method.

He smiled and responded by telling me that he was pleased I had enjoyed it, and said I was now going to be the site champion! Wow, I had only just been trained as a facilitator, and now, just after a week onsite, I was being made site champion for the RCA program. This was going to be interesting. It felt like a sink-or-swim situation. But deep down, I knew I was ready. I already knew the importance of having an effective RCA method within the reliability engineer's toolbox.

Because here's the thing, without a well-structured RCA process, failures don't get solved; they just get fixed temporarily. And when that happens, the same problems come back, again and again. Teams get frustrated, operations become reactive instead of proactive, and everyone ends up stuck in firefighting mode.

Using an effective tool like Apollo RCA, you go deeper. You get beyond the symptoms and uncover the real causes of the problem or failure, so it does not happen again.

"If you don't find and fix the causes, the problem will find you again and often with a higher price to pay."

That's why effective root cause analysis is one of the most crucial tools in our reliability journey.

It's not a step to skip. It's not something you rush. And it's definitely not just a box to tick.

It's how we prevent accidents, enhance performance, and, most importantly, keep people safe.

And so, as we close this chapter, turning down the role in Wanganui was more than just saying no to a job; it was saying yes to the chance of something better. It taught me that instinct matters, and that sometimes walking away is what creates the space for the right opportunity to appear.

Another chapter was about to begin, one that would take me deeper into the world of reliability, safety, and leadership than I had ever gone before.

*"If you don't
change
the conditions,
the story repeats."*

Chapter 4

Learning, Leading and Living in the Long White Cloud

Learning, Leading and Living in the Long White Cloud

"Opportunities don't happen. You create them."
Chris Grosser

After several years of building hands-on experience in the UK with the same company, I had now settled into life in New Zealand with my partner, Sharon. We were living in our first home in New Plymouth, and life was starting to feel really good. Sharon had been successful in getting a midwifery position at the local Taranaki Base Hospital. It was a big step for both of us, and seeing her settle into her new role made me feel even more confident about our decision to move.

As for me, I was settled into my role as a Site Reliability Engineer at Kapuni, and it felt like we were both exactly where we were meant to be. Also, after living in a few rental properties, we finally purchased our first house here, which, to be honest, needed some work and renovation, but it was full of potential. Weekends were quickly filled with DIY projects, paint-splattered overalls, and endless trips to the shops. It was hard work, but it helped us put down roots and made New Plymouth feel even more like home.

Regarding my career, this phase provided me with the opportunity to apply everything I had learned about reliability and maintenance, but in a completely new setting. The challenges were real, the environment was different, and the learning curve was steep. But it was also energising. I was ready to move beyond theory and get hands-on with real problems, in a real plant, with real consequences. And through that, I began to grow, not just professionally, but personally as well.

This chapter takes you through that journey: from navigating the day-to-day challenges at Kapuni to the professional milestones that helped shape my evolving approach to asset management. It includes the first time I facilitated an Apollo RCA, the discovery and addressing of "bad actors," the rollout of a comprehensive Reliability Centred Maintenance (RCM) program, and how tools like Weibull analysis became part of our problem-solving toolkit. More than just technical wins, this period taught me key lessons about leadership, communication, planning, and what it really takes to build a lasting culture of reliability, especially in an ageing asset base.

Looking back, this period wasn't just about applying what I knew; it was about being changed by the experience. It became a foundation for everything that would follow in my career.

And this is where the story begins...

TRUST THE PROCESS

Back onsite at Kapuni, things were also moving forward. I had started to engage with the site team of technicians, and slowly but surely, trust was being built. The Apollo RCA program was underway, and approximately 20% of my time was now dedicated to it, both managing the program and facilitating problems.

One of the first things I did was dig into the site's data, run a Pareto Analysis and identify the site's bad actors' list. Now, for anyone not familiar with that term, it's a really simple but powerful decision-making tool used to identify and focus on the most important causes of a problem. It is based on the 80/20 principle.

Also known as the 80/20 Rule, it suggests that 80% of the results come from 20% of the causes. In reliability and maintenance terms:

- 80% of downtime might come from just 20% of your assets.
- 80% of failures might be caused by 20% of failure modes.
- 80% of maintenance costs may stem from 20% of machines.

It's an excellent method to identify and prioritise the 'vital few' problems that have the most significant impact, so you don't waste time on the 'trivial many'.

The steps:

1. List problems or causes (e.g. failure types, breakdowns, delays).
2. Measure frequency or impact (e.g. downtime hours, cost).
3. Rank them in descending order.
4. Create a bar chart with causes on the x-axis and their impact on the y-axis.
5. Add a cumulative percentage line to see which causes make up 80% of the total.

It was evident from the data that the site's control valves were an issue. They were right at the top of the 'bad actors' list, and the amount of downtime was significant. This wasn't just a minor issue we could brush aside. It was costing time, money, and a lot of frustration. So, I decided this would be the perfect problem to use as my first facilitated Apollo RCA investigation onsite.

I called a team together: the site Mechanical Engineer, Process Engineer, Electrical Supervisor and Workshop Technician. I figured that this mix of people would bring the right knowledge and perspectives into the room. But I won't lie, I was nervous. It was my first Apollo RCA in front of people I was only just getting to know.

I believed in the Apollo process, but belief doesn't always take away the nerves. I kept telling myself, "Just trust the process. Follow the steps. It works." I'd said that enough times in my head that I started building my own confidence before the RCA began.

Some of these people had never even heard of the Apollo RCA before, so I prepared a few presentation slides to introduce the process. We were just getting started. I was setting the scene, about to get us all aligned on Step 1: Problem Definition, when all of a sudden, the Mechanical Engineer banged the table.

Everyone went quiet.

"Why are we wasting our time on this?" he said sharply. "I already know the solution!"

Wow, I wasn't expecting that at all. The training had not exactly prepared me for someone giving me a solution at the start of the investigation, but here I was, my First Apollo RCA, and already someone was jumping ahead to starting at Step 3: Identify Effective Solutions.

During the Apollo RCA training, we did discuss some of the causes of ineffective problem solving, and one of those causes is 'jumping to solutions', which is often seen in what we call 'solution-oriented' people.

When someone is 'solution orientated' but avoids working through a problem, it often stems from a mindset, pressure or even past experiences. I have come across this scenario time and time again throughout my career. Engineers are trained to solve problems; that's what we enjoy, it's what gives us a buzz. However, jumping directly to a solution without understanding the causes can often lead to the problems recurring again and again.

Spending time analysing a problem can feel like 'wasting time', especially if they think the solution seems obvious. This was also the case in my first Apollo RCA 'Premature Failure of Control Valves'. Time was tight, and the pressure was on. People wanted answers, fast.

As I mentioned in Chapter 2, time pressure and cultures in fast-paced environments often lead to quick decision-making and acting quickly. When we need to 'keep things moving', we can create a culture where quick fixes get rewarded, but understanding the real issue might be quietly ignored, because reflection on the problem is seen as a delay.

However, strong reliability cultures have to find the right balance between good quality problem solving and timely action with the implementation of effective solutions. So, here I was faced with a solution-oriented Mechanical Engineer. What do I do?

As a facilitator of RCAs, you are often faced with different kinds of scenarios. At that moment, I had a choice: let the meeting derail, or gently guide it back on track. I took a deep breath, kept calm, and quickly thought on my feet. I listened to the Mechanical Engineer, who had raised his voice, banged the table, and told me I was wasting time with this investigation.

The next thing I did was write down his solution. I could see that's all he wanted, someone to listen. And once I put his suggestion up on the board, you could see the tension melt away. He looked relieved. I explained we don't discuss solutions until step 3, but so we don't forget this solution, I wrote it on a yellow Post-it note and stuck it in the corner of the whiteboard.

And yes, I'll admit it, I had stepped away from the standard four-step process. But, in that moment, I was playing the role of a facilitator, and sometimes you might have to treat scenarios differently depending upon the circumstances.

Having now been facilitating RCAs for most of my career, I've seen all kinds of personalities and challenges, and I'll share more of those stories later in this book. But one question I get asked a lot, especially during Apollo RCA training, is this:

What makes someone an effective facilitator?

HERE ARE MY THOUGHTS ON WHAT MAKES AN EFFECTIVE RCA FACILITATOR:

1. Neutral and Objective
   - Doesn't take sides or assign blame
   - Creates a safe space where facts come before feelings
   - Keeps the team focused on learning, not finger-pointing "Let's focus on what happened, not who's at fault."

2. Thinks Systemically
   - Understands that most failures are system-based, not people-based
   - Looks for patterns, process gaps, or latent conditions, not just surface-level causes
   - Encourages a "zoom out" view: "What conditions allowed this to happen?"

3. Guides, Doesn't Dominate
   - Facilitates discussion instead of dictating the outcome
   - Asks open-ended questions to draw out knowledge from the group
   - Keeps the team aligned with the RCA structure

4. Strong Communication Skills
   - Keeps everyone engaged: operators, engineers, managers
   - Manages different personalities and keeps the discussion productive
   - Summarises, clarifies, and helps the team build shared understanding

5. Controls the Process & the Clock
   - Balances depth with time avoids "analysis paralysis"
   - Knows when to dig deeper and when to move on
   - Keeps the team focused on causes, then transitions to corrective actions and solutions

6. Understands the Business Context
   - Knows the asset, process, or production environment well enough to ask relevant questions
   - Links technical findings to business impact (e.g., cost, safety, downtime)

7. Follows Through
   - Ensures that corrective actions are clear, owned, and tracked
   - Doesn't let the RCA become a "talking shop"
   - Helps teams learn from the process, not just check a box

8. Promotes a Learning Culture
   - Reinforces that failure is a source of learning, not punishment
   - Helps shift the organisation from reactive to proactive
   - Champions continuous improvement, not just one-time fixes

"A great RCA facilitator doesn't just solve problems; they build problem solvers."

As I previously mentioned, my time on the RCA program accounted for approximately 20% of my overall job role.

MOVING FROM REACTIVE TO PROACTIVE MAINTENANCE

The RCA program was focusing on what had gone wrong, what had failed, what had broken down, with the expectation that solutions would be identified to prevent recurrence. Now, depending on complexity, some of these solutions can be implemented relatively quickly. But others were more complicated and could take several months before they were fully implemented.

And while we were working on those long-term fixes, there was always the risk that the same problems could crop up again in the meantime. That was frustrating, mainly because we were often fighting fires instead of proactively addressing the issues. This led me to start thinking more about prevention.

Instead of just asking, "What failed and how do we fix it?"
I started asking, "How can we stop things from failing in the first place?", especially considering the pressure from what was seen as an end-of-life asset.

That's when the conversation shifted towards the need for a more proactive approach: a proper reliability program.

We were dealing with ageing equipment, and many people saw it as being at the end of its life, but the site was running a high level of 'reactive' maintenance. The maintenance strategy had changed over time, and it wasn't always consistent or effective. The site needed a reliability program based on the principles of RCM (Reliability Centred Maintenance). At that point, someone asked the question,

"Why implement RCM on this site?"

Well, to me, the answer was simple. Implementing a structured program of RCM was going to support the site in performing the right maintenance at the right time and for the right reasons. It's about working smarter, not just harder. Since then, I've had the opportunity to implement RCM across various industries and settings, and I've seen firsthand how powerful it can be.

When done correctly, a well-structured RCM program brings several key benefits:

1. Improves Equipment Reliability

RCM focuses on understanding how and why equipment fails, so you can:

- Prevent the most likely failure modes
- Apply the most effective maintenance tasks (not just generic PMs)
- Keep critical assets running longer and more predictably

It's smarter than just fixing things when they break or changing parts "just in case."

2. Reduces Unnecessary Maintenance Costs

You stop doing:

- Overly conservative, time-based PMs that waste time and money
- Maintenance that doesn't prevent failure (a lot of it doesn't!)

Instead, RCM helps you:

- Use condition-based or predictive tasks where they make sense
- Optimise labour, spares, and downtime

You're no longer "busy being busy" - you're being effective.

3. Enhances Safety and Compliance

RCM identifies failure modes that could affect safety, quality or the environment, and makes sure the right controls are in place.
It ensures:

- You're maintaining safety-critical functions properly
- You're defensible in audits and investigations

It's not just about uptime; it's about responsible operations.

4. Builds a Better Understanding of Your Assets

RCM forces you to ask:

- What's the function of this asset?
- How can it fail?
- What happens when it does?

That process builds asset knowledge, improves training, and strengthens your maintenance and operations culture.

5. Aligns Maintenance with Business Goals

RCM links asset care directly to:

- Production output
- Quality
- Safety
- Cost

Maintenance stops being a cost centre and becomes a value enabler.

6. Creates a Foundation for Other Strategies

RCM sets the stage for:

- Condition monitoring
- Digital transformation
- Maintenance planning and scheduling
- Asset lifecycle management

Without a solid RCM foundation, those other programs often fail to deliver their full value.

The Bottom Line: "RCM is about doing maintenance that matters - no more, no less."

To make it clearer, I have also documented the 'Before vs After RCM'

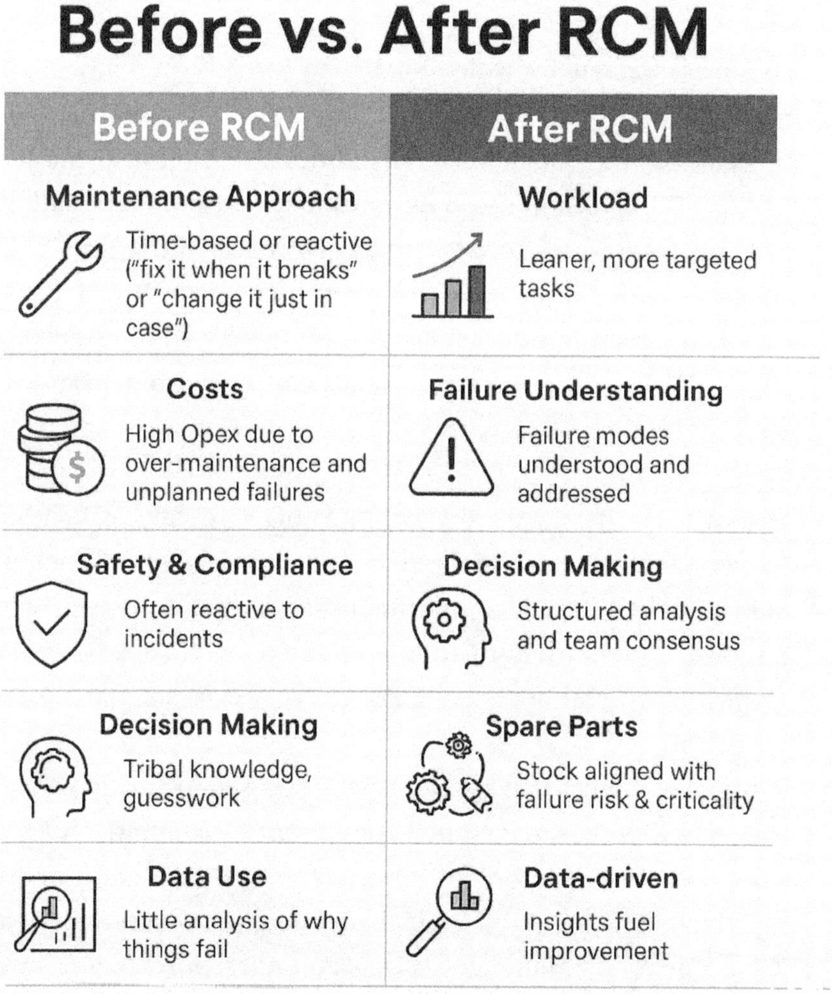

Figure 1: Before vs After RCM

As you can see from Figure 1, it's a structured, systematic way to make reliability decisions that are:

- Technically sound
- Business-aligned
- Risk-aware

Before I started my role, Shell had already purchased and installed a software called Isograph RCMCost (now known as Peak Avenue Isograph AWB). Once I settled into the job, I started exploring the software, trying to understand its functionality. And to be honest, I really did like it! Of course, with any software, you can always identify opportunities for improvement, but it was far better than the RCM Excel worksheets I had been filling out in my ICI days.

Out of curiosity, I asked where the software came from, and to my surprise, it originated in Warrington, UK. I couldn't believe I had travelled to the other side of the world to discover some software that originated only 40 miles away from where I had been using RCM Excel worksheets.

It was excellent software. I am still using it to this day. Over the years, it has developed and improved significantly. It even had a built-in Weibull Analysis tool. Back at ICI, and in my reliability training, I had been taught to use the Mean Time Between Failure (MTBF) as an indicator of failure rate.

Thinking back then was simple; if we could schedule maintenance before the failure, we would extend life and prevent unplanned downtime.

WEIBULL ANALYSIS

I also know from my experience that this didn't work all the time. Sometimes, after analysis, we would update the maintenance inspection frequency; yet, the asset would still fail before the inspection. It was frustrating, and at the time, we didn't really understand why. And now here I was learning why that was the case.

Understanding Weibull was a game-changer in my approach to maintenance optimisation. Not only is it essential to understand when something is likely to fail, but it's also important to know how something will fail. That changed the way I approached maintenance strategy optimisation. I like to keep Weibull analysis simple. I have not only used it for reliability studies and maintenance strategy optimisation, but also for investigating evidence in root cause analysis.

Weibull analysis is a powerful tool; it helps identify the nature of failures, whether they are:

- Early-life failures (infant mortality) which are often linked to fit-for-purpose or installation issues
- Random failures with a constant failure rate
- Wear-out failures that occur as assets age

Understanding these patterns really changes how you look at maintenance. When you can see the trends in the data, it allows you to optimise your maintenance approach. For example, you might increase inspections during the early life of a piece of equipment if you know it's more likely to fail early on. Or, on the other hand, you might schedule a full replacement just before the wear-out phase begins, to avoid a sudden failure.

By making data-driven decisions, you can strike the right balance: avoiding both over-maintenance and unexpected breakdowns. And optimising for the lowest cost and risk. One moment that really confirmed this for me was when I was working onsite at Kapuni. I was studying the failure history of the main oil pump in a duty-standby operation. The data indicated to me that a failure was imminent. So, I went to see our Condition Monitoring Engineer and asked if he had recently done the vibration analysis on the pump with his trusted CMVA 10 SKF vibration analyser. He told me it wasn't due for another few weeks and asked why I was asking.

I told him I was doing some data analysis and that the pump Weibull data indicated a failure was not far away.

He gave me a curious look and asked, "Have you actually been out to the pump? Have you heard it making any noise?"

Well, it was a good question, because at that point I hadn't been to the pump. So, Ian got his analyser and we went out to take a one-off vibration reading of the pump. When Ian took the reading, his reaction said it all. The pump was operating at a level higher than its warning alarm, representing a significant increase since the last reading. He was amazed.

Curious, he wanted to know how I had been so selective for that pump. That's when I showed him the Weibull analysis I had done. He was sold, and from then on, we started working together on further data sets. We carried out some spot checks on rotating equipment that had looked very close to failure.

That experience was a real turning point for me as I was also sold on the Weibull approach. But as I mentioned earlier, if you keep it simple and stick to the basics, you'll still get powerful, actionable insights that can drive better maintenance decisions. There are many textbooks and technical guides available that can make it feel overwhelming, especially for those just starting out. In some cases, the complexity can actually slow you down or even put people off from using it altogether.

That's why I've created a simple Weibull Analysis Cheat Sheet. Something straightforward, practical, and easy to use.

WHAT IS WEIBULL ANALYSIS?

Weibull analysis is a statistical tool used to model time-to-failure data and predict the failure behaviour of components or systems.

When to Use Weibull Analysis?

Use it when:

- You have time-to-failure or usage-based failure data.
- You want to:
  - Estimate reliability over time
  - Identify failure patterns (random, early-life, wear-out)
  - Predict remaining life
  - Compare the reliability of different assets or suppliers

Minimum Data Required

- At least 4–10 failure data points (more is better)
- Optionally: include suspended data (units still running when study ends)

Symbol	Name	Meaning
β (Beta)	Shape parameter	<1: Infant mortality, 1: Random, >1: Wear-out
η (Eta)	Scale parameter	Characteristic life (63.2% fail by this time)
γ (Gamma)	Location (optional)	Failure-free period (rarely used)

Table 1: Key Parameters

Interpretation Tips

- β < 1: Early failures dominate → look at design, installation, speak with OEM
- β = 1: Random failures → check operating environment, human error.
- β > 1: Wear-out → consider PM or redesign.

Weibull Plotting Steps

1. Collect failure times (and censored data if available).
2. Rank data in ascending order.
3. Apply the Weibull plotting formula or use software (we use Peak Avenue Isograph AWB software, as it links directly to the failure mode in the maintenance strategy).
4. Fit a Weibull distribution and extract β and η.
5. Assess goodness-of-fit (e.g., correlation coefficient or likelihood methods).
6. Use the model to:

   - Predict failures
   - Set maintenance intervals (for cost and risk reduction)
   - Justify redesign or spares strategy

Common Pitfalls to Avoid

- Using too little or poor-quality data.
- Assuming everything follows a Weibull distribution (check for goodness of fit).
- Ignoring mixed failure modes (e.g., wear-out + random).
- Misinterpreting β or over-relying on visual fit without stats.
- Applying results without considering the operational context.

I have multiple case studies of how and when I have used Weibull analysis in my role as a Reliability Engineer; however, I have selected the one below, which also supports a root cause analysis investigation.

Case Study
Weibull Analysis

Whilst performing an FMECA study on an asset in Tasmania, the site maintenance manager approached me to ask if I could do some analysis on the site furnace electric inductors, which had recently become problematic and had experienced several failures over the last couple of years. The data was captured, and within a couple of hours, an interesting picture had emerged.

Based on the available failure data, we were able to identify both the worst-performing and the best-performing inductors in terms of failure characteristics. Only a couple of inductors were showing wear-out-type failures. One inductor remained operational after 100,000 hours.

However, due to the high percentage of infant mortality type failures (beta < 1), I suggested conducting an RCA investigation to identify the root causes and develop solutions to extend lifespan and increase reliability.

I pointed out that 'Infant mortality' typically indicates issues related to commissioning, installation, or fit-for-purpose areas that would be covered in the RCA.

Within two weeks, the maintenance manager informed me they had run an RCA onsite with the suppliers of the inductors.

Interestingly, the supplier had made a modification to the inductors that included a thermocouple installation.

The wire used within the thermocouple was actually touching both the positive and negative elements of the inductor, which in turn caused a short circuit within the inductor and reduced its operational life.

The initial conversation with the inductor manufacturer indicated that no changes had been made, and the issue was related to how the site was installing them. But once we had the data and the analysis, we were able to use this as evidence in the RCA investigation.

Again, another example of successfully using Weibull to support an RCA.

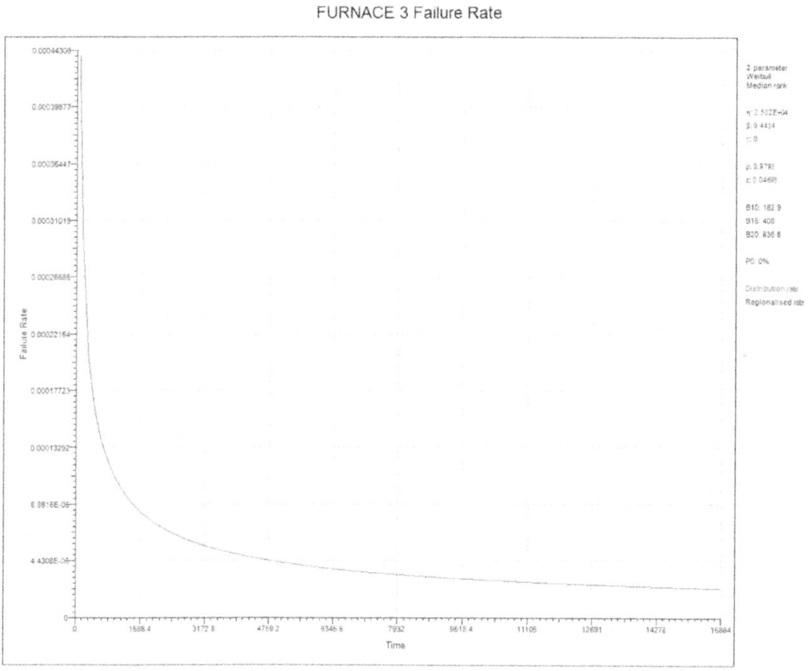

Figure 2 – Furnace 3 Weibull Parameters showing Early-Life Failure

If you're a Reliability Engineer and haven't explored Weibull analysis yet, I highly recommend you give it a try.

While some in the field remain sceptical, and the method indeed has its limitations, my experience has shown it to be an excellent tool for uncovering failure patterns and guiding smarter decisions.

Like any technique, its value depends on the quality of the data and the way it's applied.

Used wisely, and in combination with engineering judgement and other approaches, Weibull analysis becomes a powerful addition to the Reliability Engineer's toolbox.

RCM AND RCA

So, now I have two excellent tools at my disposal: RCM (Reliability Centred Maintenance) and RCA (Root Cause Analysis). They both complement each other really well. During my time at Shell New Zealand, I split my time between both activities. Eighty per cent of my time was spent on preventing future failures through RCM studies, and 20% was dedicated to managing the Apollo RCA program, where I acted as the site champion. That role involved a mixture of facilitation and program management.

A question I often get asked when delivering training courses on both topics is,

'Which comes first: the RCM or the RCA?'

It's an excellent question and definitely worth exploring. Let me break it down in a simple way.

RCM is a 'Pre-Problem Solving Methodology'. It's all about getting ahead of failures before they happen.

With RCM, you have the opportunity to:

•To record what could go wrong with your assets before it does.
•Initiate mitigating actions to prevent failures.
•Predictive and Preventive Maintenance Actions.

In contrast, RCA (Root Cause Analysis) is a 'Post-Problem-Solving Methodology'. It comes into play after something has already gone wrong.

It helps you:

•Get to the bottom of what happened and why, to prevent recurrence (reactive)
•Learn from failures in a structured way.
•It's often reactive, but it can also be used proactively, especially when minor issues start appearing that could become bigger over time.

So, which comes first?

At the end of the day, either approach can be applied first and will be dependent on the situation being faced. My advice to our own customers is: If you're currently dealing with frequent or costly failures and you're not actively managing those losses, that's the place to start. Focus on understanding what's going wrong.

Use a structured Root Cause Analysis (RCA) method, such as Apollo RCA, to thoroughly investigate the issues. This helps you identify the underlying cause of the problems, not just the symptoms. Once you've got that system in place and running well, you'll start seeing improvements.

Then, with those urgent issues under control, it's a good time to shift gears and start thinking ahead. That's where Reliability-Centred Maintenance (RCM) comes in. RCM is all about being proactive. It helps you plan and prevent future failures from happening when you least expect them.

Like Weibull, I have numerous case studies to demonstrate the use of both RCM and RCA. I selected the one below because this really demonstrates how both tools were used to address the same problem, the deterioration of Overall Equipment Effectiveness (OEE).

OEE is a standard metric used to measure how effectively a manufacturing process or piece of equipment is being utilised. It combines three factors: Availability (uptime vs. downtime), Performance (actual speed vs. ideal speed), and Quality (good products vs. defects), into a single percentage.

A score of 100% means the equipment is producing only good parts, as fast as possible, with no downtime. OEE helps organisations identify losses, improve productivity, and benchmark performance.

Case Study – OEE Loss RCA and RCM

The client had started to see a deterioration in OEE on a critical bottling line, following the installation of a new automated case packer. The main assets on the line were approximately 10 years old and had undergone various modifications over the previous few years of production.

Following a review of the production line data and interviews with various Production and Maintenance personnel, an action plan was developed to reverse the OEE decline within a 7-week operational window. A Manufacturing Improvement Team (MIT) were brought together, and a plan of action was developed. The first step was to conduct an Apollo Root Cause Analysis of the 'OEE Deterioration on the Production Line', which would identify solutions to turn around this customer-critical situation.

Following the RCA, several actions were performed:

1. Conduct a Detailed OEE Loss Review
2. Red Tag the Line
3. Perform RCA on big losses
4. Develop a Preventive Maintenance (PM) and Autonomous Maintenance (AM) program through the RCM study application
5. Develop a 'Day in the Life' of a line operator

6. Develop a Visual Management Board and associated process
7. Confirm the line capacity
8. Review the changeover process

The approach allowed the client to take control over the losses and identify solutions for increased, steady, and consistent production. It consisted of both Operational and Reliability Excellence activities that culminated in delivering the required production goal within a very short period.

The RCM study was completed in 15 days and resulted in the analysis of:

- 16 Main Assets
- 277 Failure Modes
- 275 Maintenance Tasks
- 127 AM Tasks / 148 PM Tasks

The fast track 'Manufacturing Improvement Team' was able to focus on the actual causes of the OEE losses in a structured and methodical way. The RCA provided a targeted plan that addressed the main causes of the OEE loss.

The RCM study resulted in a failure mode-driven, optimised maintenance strategy that was designed to identify and minimise the losses due to asset failure. This combined approach of RCA and RCM enabled the team not only to establish a good reliability foundation but also to break a three-year production record as an added bonus.

Chapter 5

The Reliability Engineers' Balancing Act

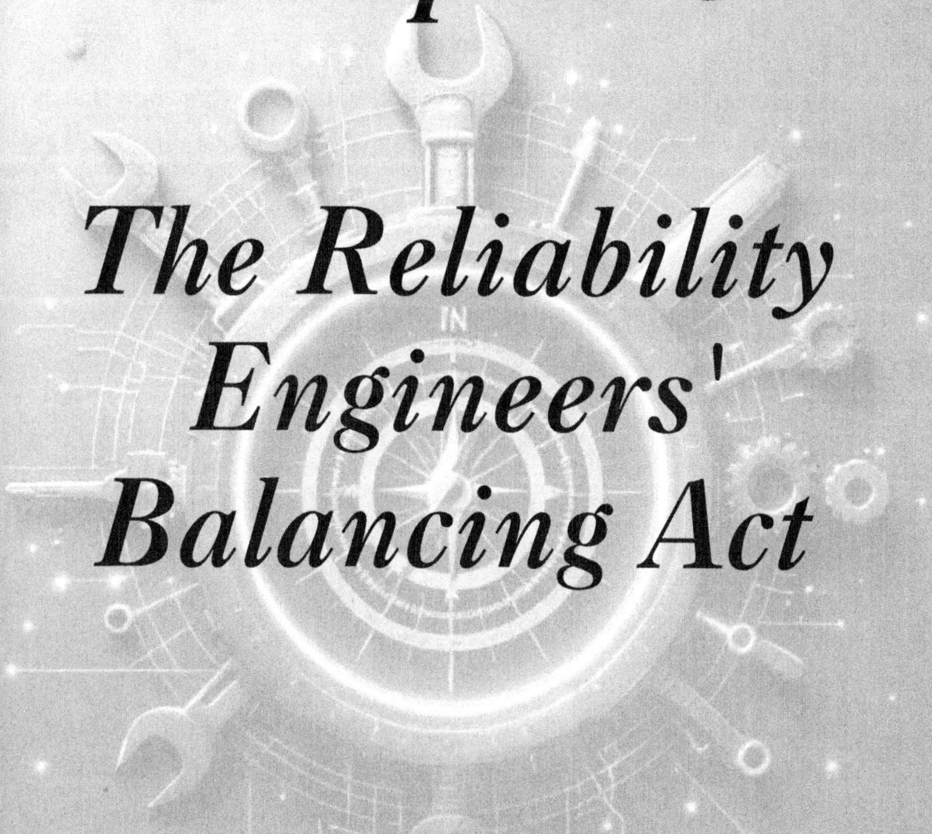

The Reliability Engineers' Balancing Act

"It is not the strongest of the species that survive, nor the most intelligent, but the one most responsive to change."
Charles Darwin

My role as a Reliability Engineer at Kapuni was going really well, and I was enjoying life in New Zealand. We had friends and family visit us from the UK and Ireland, which certainly helped alleviate the isolation of being in such a faraway place. And it is quite possibly the farthest place you can reach from the UK, not to mention it really puts the "long haul" in long-haul flights too!

We also discovered new traditions. As we drew closer to our first Christmas in the country, our friends started talking about barbeques on Christmas Day at the beach in the sunny weather, and swimming in the sea, instead of huddling by the fireplace. It was all so different from the cold, cosy Christmases we were used to back in the UK. But that was part of the adventure.

This is what we wanted to try: new things, new experiences and a completely new way of living.

But engineering has a way of reminding you that just when everything seems steady, failure can arrive unannounced. A sudden pump breakdown at Kapuni tested not only my technical skills but also the systems, processes, and culture that underpin reliability.

In this chapter, we will explore how one critical failure unfolded, what it revealed about the importance of concepts like the P-F interval and the design envelope, and how communication, planning, and execution make the difference between reactive firefighting and proactive reliability.

NOT ON THE RADAR UNTIL IT FAILED

A few weeks before Christmas, things took a sudden turn at work. We had a significant failure onsite at Kapuni. It was a regular morning. I had arrived on site at 07:30 am as usual. However, as soon as I arrived, I discovered that our main high-pressure export oil pump had failed overnight.

It was a large piston pump powered by a Waukesha gas-fired engine. Both assets were old, but up until that point, they hadn't experienced any failures or problems. According to data, they were not on the reliability radar. That said, the pump had been identified as a single point of failure during the development of a sitewide 'Reliability Block Diagram' and was deemed a critical asset.

Unfortunately, that risk had now turned into reality. The maintenance team got into action and started to strip down the pump to figure out what went wrong. Meanwhile, site production had stopped, and the transfer of oil to the tank farm had ceased. The pressure was on!

The storeman was busy, checking for stock items and spare parts associated with this pump. I had a conversation with the Condition Monitoring Engineer, and he had no history showing any pump degradation issues. I also checked in with the Process Engineer, who confirmed there hadn't been signs of performance degradation either. This appeared to be a random event with no prior warnings; everything had seemed normal, until it wasn't.

P-F INTERVALS

However, in my experience, after years of facilitating RCA investigations and performing reliability studies, most failures, however sudden, will have given some indication or early warning signs regarding the onset of a failure. In reliability, we often refer to the P-F interval. If you can spot a problem during the P-F interval, you have a chance to fix it before it leads to a breakdown. It's like a warning light on your car dashboard, you don't ignore it, because if you do, the next thing you know, you're stuck on the side of the road.

Similarly, the P-F interval, also known as the Potential-Failure interval, is a key concept in reliability and maintenance engineering. It represents the time between the point when a potential failure can first be detected (P) and the point when the asset fails (F).

Key Definitions

- P (Potential Failure Point):
- The moment when something starts to go wrong, but the asset is still functioning. This could be the appearance of a detectable symptom (e.g., vibration, heat, noise).
- F (Functional Failure Point):
- The moment when the asset can no longer perform its intended function.
- P-F Interval = F - P
- This is the window of opportunity for detecting the problem and taking corrective action before failure.

Why the P-F Interval Matters?

- It determines how often you should inspect or monitor an asset.
- To catch failures in time, inspections or condition monitoring must happen more frequently than the P-F interval.
- It's fundamental to Condition-Based Maintenance (CBM) and predictive maintenance strategies.

How is it used?

- Helps define inspection intervals in PM or CBM programs.
- Guides sensor selection and determines the monitoring frequency for predictive maintenance.
- Supports RCM (Reliability-Centred Maintenance) decision-making.

The P-F interval is your time window to detect, plan, and act before a failure causes downtime or damage. That's what proactive maintenance is all about; not waiting for things to go wrong, but spotting the signs early and stepping in before it's too late. However, in this case, the failure of our piston pump was unexpected, as there were no warning signs at all. One day it was working fine, and the next morning it had completely failed. No alerts, no alarms, no signs of distress. It just stopped. Or... did it?

That's the question I kept asking myself. Had we really been given no warning? Or had we missed something?

As the Reliability Engineer, I was immediately tasked with collecting the evidence and planning an RCA investigation. This failure was serious; production had stopped, and the pump was a known single point of failure. This one was certainly going to trigger an RCA investigation at the site.

That's where RCA trigger points come into play. Trigger points are vital as they are guidelines or thresholds, we set to help in deciding where and when to run an RCA. It could be based on cost, safety risk, downtime impact, or asset criticality. This one ticked every box. So, I started digging.

Once the pump had been stripped, the evidence of damage was in full sight. One of the pistons was bent, and there were signs of metal-to-metal contact, with bad visible scoring. We took plenty of photographs for the investigation and documented every angle, every damaged part.

During the evidence gathering for the upcoming RCA, I started to look through both the Maintenance Strategy and Operating Procedures for this pump. One thing I noticed was that, according to the date on the documented operating procedure, the operating procedure had been updated just two months before the failure.

But what exactly had changed?

It wasn't obvious which procedural information had been updated. Just a new version of the document with a more recent date on it. That raised a red flag for me. The pump had failed on the night shift, so I knew I needed to speak with the operator who was on duty at the time.
But before I could even get that far, the usual 'bun fight' had also started.

Operations was pointing the finger at Maintenance, as is often the case, even though no one really knew yet what had gone wrong. It was the same old traditional, "let's blame maintenance for the failure", simply because the asset failed.

Eventually, I got to speak to John, the night shift Operator. He was in the control room, sitting in front of the plant's HMI screens. He was a straight-talking guy who didn't mince his words. He leaned back and said, "I will tell you why it failed." He went on to say to me that the night shift now only had one control room operator, and the operator had to remain in the control room at all times.

To properly stop the transfer pump, at least according to the original operating instructions, someone needed to physically go out to the Waukesha gas engine, bring it down from 900 RPM to under 100 RPM, and only then shut off the transfer pump. John pointed out that the new operating procedure now allowed the pump to be stopped using the 'big red' emergency stop button on the wall in the control room!!!

And that's precisely what happened on the night of the failure. The pump had been stopped using the emergency stop button whilst operating at high speed. This was also the first time it had ever been stopped this way. All previous stops had occurred during the day shift when two operators were present, allowing someone to go outside and follow the correct shutdown procedure.

I managed to obtain the previous revision of the Operating Procedure, and sure enough, it contained clear instructions stating that the gas engine 'Must' be disengaged from running and the pump 'Must' be stopped at slow speed. Stopping under pressure and high speed could result in damage to the pump. And that's exactly what happened.

Wow, I couldn't believe it! This one critical instruction had been removed from the latest operating procedure two months earlier. That wasn't just surprising, it was alarming. Even more shocking was that nobody from the 'Engineering' team was aware of this operating change. This is precisely the kind of situation that the Management of Change (MoC) process is designed to prevent.

MoC is a formal process used to review, assess, and approve any changes to equipment, procedures, or operations, especially those that can impact safety, reliability, or performance. They protect people, assets, and reputation by making sure changes are deliberate, reviewed, and well-communicated, not accidental or rushed.

Had this change been implemented through an 'MoC Business Process,' the risk known to engineers would have potentially prevented this failure from occurring.

Of course, modern automation and field devices could be installed to allow the slow ramp down of the engine from the control room, but this was a redesign option that was not even on the radar. During the night shift, when there's only one operator in the control room, the only option is to press the big red emergency stop button.

That one shortcut ended up resulting in a catastrophic failure.

This situation really drove home a frustrating reality I've seen throughout my career. Maintenance departments get blamed for a high number of production losses following equipment failures.

Yet in most studies I have facilitated or taken part in, most reasons for failure or unreliability of the asset have come mainly from how the equipment is operated, not how it's maintained.

And that brings me to an important concept: the design envelope.

THE DESIGN ENVELOPE

The "design envelope" refers to the specific operating conditions, like temperature, pressure, load, speed, and environmental factors, within which the equipment is engineered to function reliably.

Operating equipment outside its design envelope introduces serious risks to reliability, safety, and performance.

It's a bit like driving a car in first gear at 100 km/h. Sure, it might go for a little while, but it won't be long before something overheats, breaks, or fails entirely. In this case, stopping the pump while it was still running at high speed was the equivalent of slamming the brakes on a speeding truck with a full load. You can imagine the damage that it can cause. It was completely outside the intended design of the system.

That's why understanding and respecting the design envelope is so critical.

To summarise, here are the key risks to reliability:

1. Accelerated Wear and Tear
   - Components experience higher mechanical or thermal stress than they were designed for.
   - Leads to fatigue, abrasion, or deformation far earlier than expected.

2. Thermal Degradation
   - Operating at higher temperatures than rated can break down lubricants, seals, or insulation.
   - Cooling systems may become inadequate, compounding failure risks.

3. Structural or Catastrophic Failure
   - Pressure vessels, rotating equipment, or load-bearing parts may fracture or explode if subjected to stresses beyond their design limits.
   - Failure is often sudden and unsafe, leaving little room for mitigation.

4. Maintenance Overload
   - Equipment outside its envelope may require frequent unplanned repairs, increasing downtime.
   - Maintenance teams are burdened with non-standard failure modes, which are harder to diagnose and fix.

5. Misleading Condition Monitoring
   - Predictive maintenance tools are calibrated for normal conditions.
   - Anomalies caused by out-of-envelope operation may be misdiagnosed or missed entirely.

6. Loss of Performance or Efficiency
   - Systems may consume more energy, produce lower output, or fail to meet quality/spec standards.

7. Safety and Compliance Violations
    - Equipment may no longer comply with safety codes, environmental regulations, or warranty terms.
    - Increases liability and risk of fines, shutdowns, or accidents.

8. Masked Root Causes
    - Chronic operation outside the design envelope normalises failure, masking the actual root causes.
    - Leads to recurring failures and wasted time on superficial fixes.

When you operate equipment outside its design envelope, you're putting the asset under stress it was never meant to take. The result? You shorten its lifespan, increase failure rates, and open the door to safety issues and compliance risks. And sometimes, the consequences don't just mean a broken part; they can mean downtime, expensive repairs, missed production targets, or even accidents that put people at risk.

So, what's the solution?

It's simple in theory but harder in practice: reliability depends on respecting design limits. If the way the equipment needs to be operated has changed, or if the old design can't keep up with new demands, then it's time to re-engineer the system to handle new conditions.

COMMUNICATE TO CULTIVATE RELIABILITY

Now, here's one area of responsibility that falls to the reliability engineer and is not always well executed: 'communication'.

Engineers are typically the 'get on and do it' type of people. They are problem-solvers. They achieve success without much fanfare; for example, they fix things, improve systems, and quietly move on to the next challenge. That's great, but it's not enough. Communication for reliability isn't just a nice-to-have; it's a must. In fact, my advice to new and existing reliability engineers is the same thing:

"Communicate, communicate, communicate."

I cannot emphasise how crucial it is for reliability engineers, managers, and teams to share their findings, document progress, and highlight successes in any site reliability initiatives.

Two key reasons why effective communication is essential:

1. Demonstrating Value to the Organisation – Reliability improvements often prevent costly failures, but since these savings are "invisible" (i.e., failures that never occurred), leadership may not fully recognise their

impact. Communicating successes helps justify investment in reliability programs.

2. Building a Reliability Culture – Sharing success stories fosters a workplace culture where reliability is valued. It encourages proactive problem-solving rather than reactive firefighting.

When I joined Shell, I brought with me something that had worked really well during my time at ICI: a simple but effective internal newsletter. So, I started producing a quarterly (every three months) newsletter focused on reliability. We set up a reliability team on site, and I encouraged others across the team to contribute to the newsletter.

We ensured the newsletter was packed with valuable and relevant information.

Some of the regular features included:

- A Bad actor Pareto - highlighting which equipment was causing the most problems
- Condition Monitoring Finds by Exception, including cost loss avoidance data
- Key RCA Findings
- A list of Upcoming training courses
- Updates on ongoing FMECA studies and status
- And a bit of inspiration, a quote of the month

The newsletter was concise and to the point, with no more than two pages, but it effectively supported the rollout of reliability initiatives across the facility.

One thing I've learned through experience, and it's something we've also highlighted in the newsletter, is that all the best reliability planning in the world means very little if you don't actually take action based on the findings. It's surprising how often people undertake RCM studies, but then fail to follow through with implementation.

Why go to all that trouble, invest in a well-structured reliability program, only to shelve the results?

You might as well not start in the first place because it's like doing half the job.

That's why execution, actually carrying out the maintenance work, is so crucial. It all comes down to proper planning and scheduling.

RESTORING BALANCE: PLANNING MAINTENANCE IN A PRODUCTION-DRIVEN WORLD

At Shell, I attended some of the planning meetings at the site to get an understanding of how maintenance was being planned and scheduled. The meetings were predominantly related to production events.

Maintenance did get a chance to speak, but ultimately, production ran the meetings, and they had the final say. As they say, Production was King. Unfortunately, this meant that maintenance requests were often pushed back or ignored. This approach was creating a big problem.

Maintenance was building a backlog to a level that was out of control AND not manageable. The planner kept having the maintenance kicked back in planning meetings, presuming it was a hopeless task. The site planner had moved into the role from working on the tools as an electrician and had not been given any formal planner training. This was evident, and the person felt he had no authority to insist on the critical PMs being delivered. It became a vicious cycle; important Preventive Maintenance (PM) tasks were repeatedly delayed, and the risk to equipment reliability continued to grow.

At the same time, something shocking was happening behind the scenes.

Someone had been poking around in the CMMS (Computerised Maintenance Management System) and had turned off hours and hours of scheduled maintenance PMs to prevent the backlog from getting any bigger. But here's what was even more shocking. It also turned out that anybody with access to the CMMS could do this.

No special permissions, no checks, no restrictions. Everybody had the same level of authority. Of course, you had to know how to turn off or cancel a maintenance PM, but nevertheless, the access levels were not managed.

All this reinforced a key point for me: A successful maintenance program isn't just about having the right strategies on paper. It's about making sure those strategies are executed properly, with support from across the business, especially from leadership.

If production always gets the final word, and maintenance is constantly sidelined, you're setting yourself up for failure in the long run.

It is crucial to ensure that the philosophy of 'Production is King' does not take over the operation of plant equipment.

To bring more structure into the management of work, especially around planning and scheduling, we arranged to set up a 'Work Management Business Process Map'.

The goal was to make the entire process more transparent, step by step, so that everyone would know exactly how maintenance tasks progressed from planning to execution.

This helped ensure the work got done on time and with fewer surprises. Personally, I am a big fan of business process maps. They really help teams get aligned and organise the approach to planning and scheduling. Creating this map wasn't something we did in isolation; we brought together a team from the site to contribute. Getting their input made a big difference because they understood the day-to-day work and challenges.

Once the map was complete and everyone had agreed on it, it became a powerful tool for us. With the new process in place, our planning and scheduling capabilities took a big leap forward.

We could now look ahead with different timeframes: five years into the future, one year, twelve weeks, and even just the weekly plan.

That level of visibility allowed us to prioritise better, reduce last-minute rush jobs, and align maintenance with production in a smarter way.

We also made changes to how we run our meetings. Instead of being led by production, the meetings were now led by the planner, which made a lot more sense for planning-focused discussions. This change came after our maintenance planners and schedulers completed training in New Zealand, which really helped sharpen their skills.

At the time, our site in New Zealand wasn't yet using the global SAP system that the rest of the company was moving toward. While SAP was definitely on the country's roadmap, we had to continue using the existing maintenance management system for a while longer.

At the end of the day, the CMMS is one key location for the reliability engineer to collect their data. The system had already undergone one CMMS transfer years earlier, and when the RCM studies began, it was discovered that some critical equipment was missing from the current CMMS.

To fix this, we went back to the basics. We used the site P&IDs (Plant Piping and Instrumentation Diagrams) and physically walked the lines. We checked each piece of equipment against what was listed in the CMMS and made corrections where needed.

It was a time-consuming process, but absolutely necessary to ensure our system had accurate and complete data.

A COMPUTERISED MAINTENANCE MANAGEMENT SYSTEM

A Computerised Maintenance Management System (CMMS) plays a critical role in supporting a company's reliability journey by serving as the central hub for data, planning, and execution of reliability-focused activities. For a CMMS to be truly supportive of this journey, it needs to do more than just schedule work orders; it must also provide comprehensive support throughout the process. A CMMS on its own will not improve asset reliability.

Over the years, I have transitioned from using a T-Card system, Excel sheets, and various CMMS systems available on the market. If I were selecting a CMMS for my own organisation, with 'reliability' being one of the key business drivers, there are several essential features I'd look for. As mentioned above, a good CMMS should do more than just manage work orders; it should support a full reliability strategy, help reduce downtime, and provide data-driven insights. Here's what criteria I would be looking for:

1. Asset Management
   - Asset hierarchy is clearly defined (systems > subsystems > components).
   - Criticality ranking is applied to all assets.
   - Asset master data includes specs, manufacturer, serial number, etc.
   - Assets are linked to location and functional context.

2. Failure Data and Analysis
   - Standard failure codes are implemented (e.g., problem-cause-remedy).
   - Failure data is consistently captured in work orders.
   - CMMS supports bad actor identification and failure trend analysis.
   - RCA tools or data exports are available for analysis.

3. Maintenance Strategy
   - PM tasks are clearly documented and linked to specific failure modes.
   - System supports all maintenance types (corrective, preventive, predictive, condition-based).
   - PM effectiveness is reviewed using historical data.
   - Predictive maintenance technologies are integrated or connected.

4. Work Management
   - Work requests can be submitted and tracked easily.
   - Work orders are prioritised based on risk and criticality.
   - Planning and scheduling tools are integrated and in use.
   - Work order closeout includes accurate failure and repair detail capture.

5. Performance Monitoring
   - Key reliability metrics are tracked (e.g., MTBF, MTTR, % planned vs reactive).
   - PM compliance and schedule adherence are monitored.

- Reports and dashboards support data-driven decisions.

6. System Integration
   - CMMS integrates with ERP and purchasing systems.
   - Condition monitoring tools and sensors feed data into CMMS.
   - Real-time alerts or alarms can trigger work orders.

7. Knowledge and Documentation
   - Work procedures and safety protocols are attached to work orders.
   - Historical data is searchable and complete.
   - Lessons learned and RCA outcomes are documented.

8. Mobility and Accessibility
   - Mobile access is available for technicians.
   - Field users can enter data and close work orders in real time.
   - Offline capabilities are supported where needed.

9. Continuous Improvement
   - Backlog analysis and Pareto of failures are reviewed regularly.
   - CMMS supports tracking of defect elimination efforts.
   - The system helps drive continuous improvement in asset performance.

Over time, a CMMS should evolve from a scheduling and

record-keeping tool into a data-driven decision support system. That's when it becomes a true asset. It becomes an enabler of reliability when it's used not just for compliance but as a strategic platform for asset health management and risk reduction.

SAYING YES TWICE: ONCE TO ADVENTURE, ONCE TO LOVE

During my last few months working at Shell Kapuni, something unexpected and exciting happened. Something that would shift the direction of both my career and my personal life. It started with a phone call from Mick Drew, the CEO of ARMS reliability, the same company that had provided us with the Apollo RCA training. I had met Mick before at one of their marketing events in New Plymouth, and we'd had a few good conversations since then. As it turned out, he and his family were coming to New Zealand for a skiing holiday, and he gave me a call to ask if I'd like to join them, along with a few other ARMS team members, for a weekend on the slopes.

As someone who had missed their usual ski trip with friends in Europe, I didn't need to be asked twice. I jumped at the chance to go skiing again. I met Mick and his family at the ski resort near Mount Ruapehu, and it turned out to be a great weekend, filled with lots of skiing, laughs, and great company.

On one evening, and after a few late-night whiskies in the hotel bar, Mick casually asked me, "Would you be interested in working in Australia?"

It caught me off guard a little. Neither Sharon nor I had seriously considered moving again at that point. We absolutely loved New Zealand. But I also wasn't about to close the door on what sounded like a new experience. So, I gave him an honest answer:

"Anything's possible. We love it here, but we're always open to travel and new adventure." That conversation was the beginning of something new.

Mick invited Sharon and me to come and visit them in Ocean Grove, a beautiful coastal town in Victoria, Australia, for a long weekend. He suggested we check them out, visit the ARMS office, get a feel for the place, and see where the discussion takes us.

And that's exactly what we did. Sharon and I flew over to Australia, and we spent a few days in Victoria. And we liked it. Yes, we loved New Zealand, but after three years, we decided to move across the pond and continue our personal adventure, as well as my own journey of reliability in Australia.

We were curious, ready for change, and saw the move as the next exciting chapter.

However, it was a risk; I had never worked for a small company before. It was a leap. But after a few conversations and working out a fair employment package, we decided to say yes. We began planning our move to Australia. But before we could pack our bags and start the next chapter of our lives in Australia, there was one more important journey we had to make, one that meant the world to both of us.

We were heading back to Ireland, to County Donegal, to Sharon's home village tucked away in the beautiful, quiet countryside. This trip wasn't about work or career plans; this was for something much more personal and meaningful: our wedding.

We had gotten engaged not long before, after a quiet and romantic beach proposal in Fiji, one of those unforgettable moments you carry with you forever. And now, we were off to celebrate that love in the heart of her homeland. She's my rock, the love of my life, and standing there in that small village church, surrounded by our loved ones, I felt deeply grateful. It was one of those moments when everything else fades away, and you realise what really matters in life.

Getting married into a new culture, with a different language (Irish Gaelic), traditions, and religion, it was always going to be a beautiful challenge. It tested us, but it also deepened our connection. But that story... well, I'll save it for another book. Maybe.

Chapter 6

Kia Ora Aotearoa, G'Day Australia

Kia Ora Aotearoa, G'Day Australia

"You can't go back and change the beginning, but you can start where you are and change the ending."
C.S. Lewis

Leaving New Zealand was never going to be easy. Sharon and I had built a life there, our first home, our first real sense of settling into a new country, and a community that felt like family. But sometimes, life has a way of nudging you forward just when you start to get comfortable. For us, that nudge came in the form of a new opportunity, one that would take us across the Tasman Sea to a place that promised sunshine, beaches, barbecues, and a whole new set of professional and personal adventures.

Australia.

This chapter picks up as we said goodbye to New Zealand (the land of the long white cloud) and set our sights on Australia (the land down under). What followed was a blend of culture shock, career progression, spider encounters (yes, really), and a fast-track introduction to the unique flavour of Australian life, equal parts laid-back and utterly unpredictable.

From my first nerve-wracking conference presentation in the Gold Coast to building a sitewide RAM model in Townsville, this chapter captures our transition into a new country, new challenges, and a new phase in my reliability journey. It also marks a turning point in how I saw myself, not just as a Reliability Engineer, but as someone who could step up, share knowledge, and thrive under pressure.

So here it is: the next leg of the journey, from Kiwi calm to Aussie chaos and everything in between.

GARY'S GUIDE TO NOT DYING IN AUSTRALIA

Well, here we are, in the land of sunshine, beaches, barbecues... and a casual abundance of creatures that want you dead. I'm talking about snakes, spiders, jellyfish, sharks, crocodiles......Seriously, this is a country where even the wildlife has an attitude.

Back home, our biggest daily crisis is about losing Wi-Fi. In Australia? You lose your shoe, because it now belongs to a spider the size of a salad plate. And I'm not even exaggerating.

Let me tell you about the day I had my first real face-to-face, or more accurately, face-to-eight-eyes contact with an Aussie spider. It happened at a quiet motel in a place called Tannum Sands near Gladstone in Queensland. Sounds peaceful, right?

I had just got out of the shower and walked back into the bedroom to get ready for a busy day at the local Aluminium Smelter, where I was performing a reliability study on the new ingot casting line. I walked back into the bedroom, I casually looked up, and there it was. I saw this giant spider on the wall. Just chilling. This thing was massive. We're talking big enough to hold a coffee mug and ask how your day's going. I initially froze as I had never seen a spider so big. But then, slowly, very slowly, I moved backwards across the room, without taking my eyes off it.

I kept thinking in my head, "How fast could the spider move? Could it possibly jump on me?"

I bent down slowly and picked up my shoe from the floor, carefully, quietly, all without taking my eye off this spider. With a shoe in hand, I then ran at speed and hit it so hard with the base of my shoe that it made the room vibrate. And the wall? Let's just say... it wasn't pretty. Now, I'm not someone who enjoys killing spiders or any living creature.

But this was life or death.

I mean, I'm in Australia and spiders kill you here, and in that moment, it was either the spider or me. Only one of us was going to survive this duel. I quickly got dressed and headed down to reception to report this near-death experience and, of course, the mess I had left across the wall.

The lady at the reception did not look impressed. She followed me back to the room, she took one look at the spider's remains and turned to me with a frown, and told me, "It was a 'Huntsman' spider", and I said, "Yeah, yeah, it was a big one!" and she then told me, "They are harmless!"

I looked at her in disbelief, I said, "You mean that could not possibly have killed me?"

"Nope", she said, "They are harmless and in fact they help keep other spiders and bugs out of the room."

I felt genuinely awful after that spider incident. I'd gone full gladiator on a creature that, in hindsight, was looking for a quiet corner. From that moment on, I promised myself that any future interactions with spiders would be treated with a bit more patience and understanding, rather than the kill first, ask questions later' approach.

Before arriving in Australia, I also knew we (The Brits) also had a healthy sporting rivalry with the Aussies (they love to beat us Poms in every sport). They call it 'sledging.' We call it 'banter.' But I hadn't realised how strong that rivalry was until I was living amongst them. The Australians hate losing to the English in cricket or rugby, and honestly, who can blame them? After all, it's not just a game, it's centuries of colonial resentment wrapped in a leather ball and a whistle.

You see, to the Aussies, beating England is like finally getting one over on your old school headmaster, the one who lectured you in Latin while confiscating your cricket bat. And to us Brits? Well, beating Australia is like tidying the empire's attic and finding out your most rebellious colony still can't quite handle losing gracefully.

They say sport builds character. In England, it mostly builds hope followed by heartbreak, but if we beat the Aussies, we'll dine out on it for decades. Just ask anyone still talking about the Rugby World Cup 2003." Thanks, Johnny Wilkinson, you legend, is still etched into pub walls across the UK.

So, at this point in the book, I thought based on my time in Australia and if you are considering a move there, well, I've documented some brief survival tips.... let's call it 'Gary's Survival Guide to Australia' (or the GSGA, who doesn't love a good acronym?)

Are you ready to dive in? Think of this less like a strict rulebook and more like a friendly nudge from someone who's learned a thing or two the hard way.

With that in mind, let's crack open the GSGA.

GARY'S SURVIVAL GUIDE TO AUSTRALIA

Spiders: The Eight-Legged Landlords

Your new house comes with tenants = free of charge. They're big, hairy, and hang in your shower like they pay rent.

- The Huntsman: It looks like it bench-presses kangaroos, but don't worry, it's "harmless," they say, as it scuttles across the ceiling like Satan on rollerblades.
- Redback Spider: Small, venomous, hides in your shoes. Think of it as a surprise sock warmer... with fangs.

Survival tip #1: Shake everything. Towels, Curtains, Spouses. Especially the shoes.

Snakes: Your Unexpected Garden Tools

Australian snakes are like overly nosy neighbours, they show up uninvited and don't leave easily.

- You'll be told, "Most of them are harmless!" That's Aussie code for: "There's a 50/50 chance this thing will kill you before you finish your sandwich."
- You learn fast that a garden hose shouldn't hiss.

Survival tip #2: If it's long, moving, and isn't a USB cable, walk away slowly and re-evaluate your life choices.

Crocodiles: Australia's Way of Saying "Stay Out of the Water".

In the tropical north, if the ocean doesn't kill you, the rivers will.

- "She'll be right," they say, as you stand next to a sign that literally reads: DO NOT SWIM. SALTWATER CROCODILES PRESENT.
- You realise quickly that "No worries, mate" actually means "Worry a lot, but pretend you're cool."

Survival tip #3: Just stay out of all water, ocean, rivers, billabongs and swimming pools.

Ants: Even the ants are aggressive. Some are called bulldog ants (yes, really). Others are fire ants.

Survival tip #4: If you see an ant offering you a handshake, do not engage; just run.

Sharks: See survival tip #3

Surviving being beaten by the AUSSIES in Sport:

Surviving Aussie sporting banter as an Englishman in Australia? It's not for the faint-hearted; it's a full-contact sport in itself. But here's to keeping your chin up, while keeping your dignity (mostly) intact:

Survival Tip #5: Learn to Smile Through the Pain.

Every time England loses in cricket or rugby (which is, let's face it, often), you'll be greeted at work with a grin and a "How bout them Poms, eh?"
Just smile. Say, "We're just letting you have a turn; it builds character." Then excuse yourself to cry privately into a cup of Earl Grey.

Survival tip #6: Master the art of the comeback.

They'll say: "Mate, we smashed you in the Ashes!"
You say: "Congratulations! Remind me again how your football team did at the World Cup?" Then run. Quickly.

Survival tip #7: Blame the weather.

If all else fails, just say, "Of course we're no good here, it's 40 degrees, everything's on fire, and I'm sweating in places I didn't know existed. No wonder we can't win, we're trying not to melt."

Survival tip #8: Be the noble loser.

Australians secretly admire someone who can take a beating with a bit of humour and grace. Bonus points if you can quote Monty Python while doing it.

Survival tip #9: Distract them with clichés.

When they start talking non-stop about sport (and they will), just yell something like, "Is that a kangaroo in the car park?" or ask if they've seen Home and Away recently. Or, when all else fails, mention the weather forecast. Trust me, these tricks work 50% of the time...every time.

Now, yes, it's true that Australia is home to 9 out of 10 of the world's most venomous snakes, and they do beat us a lot in sports. But, there's way more to Australia than deadly creatures and ruthless cricket teams. It also has Tim Tams (awesome chocolate biscuits), excellent wine, great food and wonderful people.

So, if you're thinking about moving to the land Down Under, go for it. It's not perfect all the time; no place is, but most days, I have no doubt you will love it. Most of the time.

FROM CLITHEROE TO THE CONFERENCE STAGE

I was fortunate that my very first day at work began with attending the ARMS annual reliability conference on the Gold Coast, Australia. How cool was that? Day one of a new job, and I am at a conference on the Gold Coast, a place people usually go for holidays. What a way to begin. Even better, my wife Sharon came with me, which made it feel like a working holiday.

We got to meet other members of the ARMS team and even their family members. Everyone was welcoming and friendly, which made the whole experience less intimidating.

The week itself was packed. There were speeches, training sessions and a good mix of social events. The social events were based around golf. Now, here's the thing: I'm not much of a golfer. I gave it a go back in New Zealand, but honestly, trying to hit a small round ball into a hole 18 times really did not appeal to me. I always thought it was a good walk ruined. Or as Robin Williams once said, "Scotland's revenge on the World". Couldn't agree more.

Now, I had been requested by Mick, the CEO of ARMS, to write and present a paper for the conference. Gulp! Present at a conference, me? This was my first day. I had not done this before. I didn't mind standing and presenting in front of a small group of people I know, but now I was being asked to present in front of maybe 100 – 150 people whom I have never met.

Needless to say, I was nervous going to the Gold Coast. I had practised and practised my paper; my poor wife, Sharon, was an absolute legend. She listened to me practice over and over again until she practically memorised the whole thing herself. On arrival, I saw the conference official program, oh no, oh....no!!!, I was looking at the itinerary, and I was the second speaker on day 1.

I was following the Keynote Speaker – Mr Dean Gano from Apollo Root Cause Analysis and author of the book, 'A New Way of Thinking'. Awesome book, highly recommended!

My stomach dropped. I suddenly felt hot and sweaty, and that wasn't the usual Gold Coast sun causing it; my nerves would surely get the better of me. I couldn't believe it was my first day at work, and less than two hours in, I was on stage talking about failure data. Oh, and I had to follow a keynote speaker who no doubt was going to be an excellent speaker!

I sat there watching Mr Dean Gano deliver his keynote, and honestly, it was awesome. You could tell he had done this before. He spoke with confidence, clarity, and a calm that made everyone in the room lean in. Dean is a very well-educated individual who has studied philosophy, religion and is a master of cause and effect. Then I heard the applause for Dean, and then came the words I dreaded:

"We'll take a short break now, and next up, our very own new team member..."

I had some water; my mouth was so dry, and I was up next on stage. That's me. Great. Imposter syndrome was kicking in. I hadn't heard of imposter syndrome at this point, but looking back, I know that's what I had.

I kept asking myself:

"Was I good enough to be presenting?
"Why was I here?"
"Why was I presenting?"
"Why didn't we stay in New Zealand?"
"I'm an ex-ICI Apprentice Maintenance Technician from Clitheroe, Lancashire, and here I am about to present at an international conference on the Gold Coast in Australia.... how did this happen...?"

Just before the morning break was over, Mick, the CEO, approached and casually asked me what I thought of the two extra slides he had added to my slide deck..." Excuse me? What slides???" I blinked. Surely, I'd misheard.

"What slides? What do they say?" I quickly asked.

"Oh, I thought I had told you?" Mick said it was like no big deal.

Not a word! He had not said a word! I was now ready to present my first paper at my first conference, and just like that, panic turned into full-blown chaos inside my head.

The bell rang. Morning break was over. Time to head back into the conference room. Mick gave me a quick nod and said, "Good luck!"

I laughed nervously and muttered under my breath, “Luck! I needed more than good luck now; I needed a miracle to happen!!”. I had practised and practised, and I knew what slides were coming, how long the presentation was going to take, well, now I had two mystery slides inserted somewhere in my slide deck! What the hell? I could feel my heart thumping in my chest.

This was my worst nightmare.

And then I heard, “And now we would like to welcome Gary Tyne, our new Reliability Engineer and team member, onto the stage to deliver his talk on ‘Data Collection and Analysis in the Oil and Gas Industry’. Please give him a round of applause.”

I could see people clapping, but oddly, I couldn’t hear the applause. The only thing I could hear was Mick's voice in my head: "What did you think of the two new slides?"

Suddenly, I noticed the crowd were looking at me. It took me a second to realise I had to quickly position myself so I could see the slides on the screen. As I waited for the mystery slides to appear, I half hoped Mick was joking with me. Maybe he was testing me on my first day to see how I would cope under pressure.

And trust me, this was real pressure!

Then, out of nowhere, the first surprise slide appeared. I don't know how fast you can read under pressure, but at that moment, I discovered I had a new skill, which is called speed reading! I'm pretty sure I only read the first and last letter of each word, and somehow, my brain automatically filled in the gaps.

I made it through that slide, barely taking a breath, and now I had to wait for mystery slide two. And when that appeared, I did the same thing. Before I knew it, I had reached the end of my presentation. I wrapped it up with a few questions and answers, and this time, when I was given a round of applause, I could actually hear it. And wow, what a relief. I was breathing again.

As I stepped off that stage, I was super proud of myself. I had delivered my first presentation, thrown a last-minute curveball, and somehow managed to pull it off. It was well received, the pressure didn't break me, and most importantly, I survived.

I told Mick, my new boss, afterwards, "Please never do that to me again!"

I honestly don't think I would survive a second episode like that. He just laughed, of course. But hey, that was my first conference speaking gig. Ironically, I am writing this chapter on a flight to Istanbul, Turkey.

I am presenting a paper at a maintenance conference in that beautiful city this week. It's hard to believe how far I've come since that nerve-racking day on stage. I have been presenting papers at conferences steadily for several years now. I've given presentations in Thailand, the USA, the UK, Ireland, Australia, Spain, and now Turkey.

I've really grown to love the experience. I enjoy sharing stories, lessons learned, and practical advice from the field. But what I enjoy just as much is the opportunity to network and help others who are either engaged in a current reliability journey or about to embark on one. I also attend other conference presentations, and I am learning equally as much. That's the beauty of this field: it keeps evolving.

Investing in yourself and learning new skills is crucial. For any new reliability engineers or graduates who may be reading this book, consider attending maintenance and reliability conferences annually. These events are packed with valuable insights, real-world case studies, and practical takeaways. The reliability community is one of the most welcoming groups I've ever come across. You'll feel right at home.

And here's one simple tip to get real value from a conference: write down three specific things you're going to try when you get back to work. Just three.

They don't have to be massive changes; it could be a new tool, a process tweak, or even a conversation you want to start with your team. The point is to take something from the experience and turn it into action. That's how continuous improvement really happens.

After that first Gold Coast conference, I spent a few months working from the small ARMS office above a bank in Ocean Grove, Victoria. It was a charming little seaside town. Some of the team would walk down to the beach at lunchtime in their boardshorts and thongs (They are sandals for those of you reading in the UK) for a quick surf. I was always invited to join, but I have to admit that my fear of sharks would not allow it. Still, it was such a beautiful part of Australia.

Eventually, ARMS had opened an office in Brisbane, and I was asked if I would like to be located there. Both Sharon and I had a chat, and we eventually decided to head to Brisbane, Queensland. I had never lived in a large city before, so I was looking forward to the experience. We rented a new apartment near the botanical gardens and started to embrace city life.

We already knew a couple of people in Brisbane, including a couple I had met in Austria years earlier, during a ski trip. We reached out to them, and they were brilliant, showing us around, and they introduced us to life in what the locals fondly call "Brissy."

Now, I don't really want to mention winning the rugby World Cup again in 2003, but this is where we were living at the time. We watched the Australia vs England World Cup final at the 'Pig and Whistle' pub on Eagle Street. What a party that was. The place was packed, the atmosphere electric. And then, that moment when Johnny Wilkinson's last-second drop kick will stay with me forever. Not to mention the huge disappointment written on the faces of those Australians in the pub. I tried to feel sorry for them, but just couldn't. But I did try, though.

SUNBURNT SKIES AND SUDDEN STORMS

Whilst we were still settling in Brisbane, an opportunity came up through ARMS to place an engineer on a six-month secondment at a Nickel Refinery in Townsville, up in Far North Queensland. And I was asked if I'd be interested in being that embedded engineer. After a bit of thought and a chat with Sharon, we decided to go for it.

This wasn't a problem as we hadn't really settled into 'Brissy' and the opportunity to live in the tropical north sounded good. Townsville was classified as the tropical part of Australia and was also the point where the crocodile's territory officially starts. That was slightly unnerving, I won't lie, but the idea of living somewhere completely different was exciting.

What stood out to us almost immediately upon our arrival in Townsville was how much more we began to learn about the First Nations peoples of Australia. Living in Far North Queensland gave us a deeper connection to the country's history, and we began to understand more about the Traditional Owners of the land on which we were now living. In the Townsville area, the Aboriginal nations include the Wulgurukaba, Bindal, Girrugubba, Warakamai, and Nawagi peoples, each with their own rich culture, stories, and connection to the country.

The more we learned, the more we realised just how profoundly sad and painful the history of colonisation has been for Aboriginal and Torres Strait Islander peoples.

When the British arrived in 1788, they declared the land terra nullius, meaning "nobody's land", completely ignoring the fact that Aboriginal peoples had lived there for over 60,000 years with rich cultures, complex societies, and deep spiritual ties to the land.

Sadly, the legacy of colonisation continues to impact Indigenous communities today, with many Indigenous Australians still facing significant gaps in health, education, and life expectancy compared to non-Indigenous Australians. Interestingly, Captain James Cook also visited the Townsville region on his first voyage to Australia in 1770, although he didn't actually land there.

While navigating this part of the Australian coast, he named the small island across from Townsville, 'Magnetic Island', as he described a magnetic pull interfering with his vessel's compass that appeared to emanate from the island. It sits just across the water from the main beach strip in Townsville.

Speaking of the beach strip, we were lucky enough to have an apartment rented for us right on the 'Strand', which is the main sea front strip in Townsville. We had a balcony with incredible sea views looking straight out toward Captain Cook's Magnetic Island. Wow, this was going to be a special secondment. Honestly, it felt like we were on a working holiday. It was one of those rare times in life when work and lifestyle lined up just perfectly.

Sharon was also able to find work in Townsville, and together we embraced life in the tropics. We used to walk the 'Strand' every evening, watching the sun go down, enjoying the sea breeze and palm trees. We even purchased some bicycles to go out cycling, and so we could explore further. One evening, I cycled to a place called Pallendra, a coastal suburb located a bit further out. There was a little shop nearby where I used to get my water bottle refilled. However, on this particular evening, something was off. They were not allowing anyone into the shop.

Curious and a bit thirsty, I asked what was going on.

Then someone casually told me that they were waiting for the local snake catcher to arrive. Apparently, two baby brown snakes had been found in the shop, and they were concerned because they didn't know where the mother snake was hiding.

"Brown snakes?", I said, suddenly forgetting I was thirsty at all. "I'm out of here!"

And yes, for those unfamiliar, brown snakes are venomous and can kill. Not exactly the kind of wildlife encounter I was hoping for on a relaxing evening bike ride. Let's just say, I cycled away faster than I've ever done before and probably broke a personal best.

We had arrived in Townsville in April, and honestly, it felt like paradise. Blue skies, warm sun, sea breezes; it was absolutely stunning. That was... until November rolled around. We hadn't seen any rain since April, and then one morning we woke up and it felt like someone had turned on the oven. The humidity was intense, and the rain started to pour. In fact, the downpour was incredible, and wow, I had never seen rain like this; it was intense!

I do apologise, but I must write about the weather in Australia. It's just something you can't ignore. Australians love talking about the weather more than I ever thought possible.

I always thought the English liked to discuss the weather, but the Aussies take it to a new level (I hope my friend John Donnelly, from Snowy Hydro, reads this; he'll know exactly what I mean!).

Australian weather is like a soap opera with no script. One minute it's blazing sunshine and blue sky; the next, you're being pelted by golf ball-sized hail while a spider the size of your fist watches from the barbecue.

In Melbourne, Victoria, you can experience all four seasons in a single hour, and still not be dressed appropriately for any of them. In Queensland, the humidity is so thick you could butter toast with it. And in the Outback? It's so hot and sunny, even the flies wear sunglasses.

The weather forecast usually goes: "Hot. With a chance of fire. Or floods. Or sharks on the highway, depending on the postcode."

Honestly, Australian weather isn't the climate. It's a gladiator arena. If you're visiting, bring sunscreen and a raincoat. And maybe a canoe! It really can be crazy!

AUSTRALIAN CULINARY DELIGHTS

On another trip to Tannum Sands, Queensland, I got a knock at my motel room door. I answered the door, and to my surprise, it was Mick (ARMS CEO) who was also in the area doing some business. He had a 6-pack of cold beers and something wrapped up in paper in his hands.

He asked, "Have you had dinner yet?" to which I replied, "I hadn't."

He then said, 'I've got some beers and mud crab here if you are hungry?'

So, we went and sat on a picnic table nearby for some beers and mud crab. I had eaten crab before and do enjoy seafood, but my crabs had always been dressed and ready to eat. My eyes could not believe it when Mick opened the paper to find a couple of fierce-looking Mud crabs just sitting there like he had just wrestled them from the ocean.

The Australian mud crab is a creature that looks like it was designed in a pub after several pints. They have massive claws, a bad attitude, and a face that says, "Come at me, mate." This isn't your dainty seafood platter crab. This is the thug of the tidal flats, a prehistoric brute with armour plating and the crushing power of a small car door.

Mick just said, 'Get stuck in!'

Mmmm. How exactly do we eat these brutes? And that's when we started pulling at the legs and sucking out the meat, breaking the main body shell and getting access to what I can only describe as absolutely delicious. This was a real Aussie culinary experience. Fresh mud crab and a 6-pack of cold beers. What a lovely surprise!

I'll also never forget the first time I ate kangaroo. I was on a trip to Port Douglas in North Queensland with Sharon, celebrating our wedding anniversary. We sit down in the restaurant; I open the menu... and there it is: "Chargrilled Kangaroo Fillet, served medium rare with bush pepper sauce."

I did a double-take. The national emblem? The thing on the coins? The one that punches tourists and boxes dogs. That kangaroo?

Now, don't get me wrong, I'm all for trying new things. But I wasn't entirely sure whether eating a kangaroo was cultural immersion... or grounds for deportation. Naturally, I ordered it.

When it arrived, it looked surprisingly respectable. Nicely seared, pink in the middle, sitting proudly next to a pile of chips that, frankly, looked a little intimidated.

I took a bite, and you know what?

It was delicious. Lean, rich, somewhere between venison and beef. Packed with flavour. Not gamey at all. My taste buds were having a party, even if the patriotic side of my brain was still waving a tiny apology to the Commonwealth.

One of the Aussie waiters saw my expression and grinned.

"Told ya, mate. It's what keeps us fit. Eat the fast ones, keep the rest sharp."

I later found out they also eat emu, the other half of their coat of arms. Only in Australia can you proudly display your national identity and also serve it with a side salad.

So, if you ever find yourself starting fresh in Australia, my advice is this: soak up the lifestyle, laugh at the banter, and learn to live alongside the local wildlife, but don't forget that the real test often happens at work.

For me, out here, it isn't just about surviving spiders or snakes; it's about navigating expectations, KPIs, and a culture that measures success in ways that might surprise you.

And that's exactly where Chapter 7 begins, learning how to survive not just the great outdoors, but also the workplace scoreboard.

*"Good endings aren't luck;
they're maintenance,
small inspections of self,
timely adjustments,
and
the courage to
replace
what no longer serves."*

Chapter 7

Metrics, Microphones & Midnight Feeds

Metrics, Microphones a & Midnight Feeds

"Resilience is accepting your new reality, even if it's less good than the one you had before,"
Elizabeth Edwards.

Reliability isn't just about machines and numbers; it's about truth and the way people and processes come together to keep a system running. In industries like mining, refining, and energy, a single overlooked failure can cost millions, risk safety, and erode trust across entire teams.

That's why Key Performance Indicators (KPIs) are so important. They're more than just performance measures; they influence culture. When applied with integrity, KPIs can expose weaknesses, support smarter maintenance strategies, and inform stronger design decisions. Misused, they can paint a picture of success while masking the seeds of future disaster. This chapter explores how reliability thinking takes root in practice, from building complex reliability models to uncovering the hard truth behind falsified KPIs to embedding reliability principles into the very design of new assets. At its core, it shows that real reliability is not about appearances; it's about integrity, foresight, and building systems (and cultures) that last.

THE RELIABILITY BLOCK DIAGRAM

My first role at the Nickel refinery in Townsville was to develop a site-wide RAM model, which stands for Reliability, Availability, and Maintainability. In simple terms, this meant I had to build something called a 'Reliability Block Diagram' (or RBD for short).

Ironically, my manager at the Nickel Refinery was a Yorkshireman named 'Andy' who had been living in Townsville for several years with his wife. The fact that I was from Lancashire meant we had some interesting conversations and rivalry from back home in England, but here, we stuck together as Englishmen in a foreign country. Andy became a good friend, and we are still in contact today.

The Reliability Block Diagram project was estimated to be a 60-day exercise, designed to model each area of the factory and determine which areas contributed to the largest unavailability losses. With those identified, the next step would be to perform RCM on the assets that impact overall plant availability.

So, what is a Reliability Block Diagram?

A Reliability Block Diagram (RBD) is a visual tool used to model the reliability of a system by showing how individual components or subsystems contribute to the overall system reliability.

Here's a simple way to explain it: Imagine your system is like a chain of blocks, each block is a component. If one block fails, depending on how the blocks are arranged, the whole system may fail or keep running.

The RBD maps out these relationships.

Key Features:

- Series Configuration: If one component fails, the whole system fails, like old Christmas lights.
- Parallel Configuration: The system functions as long as one path is operational. Think backup generators.
- Mixed/Complex Configurations: Most real systems combine series and parallel paths.

Why it's useful:

- Helps calculate system reliability based on the reliabilities of its components.
- Assists in design decisions, e.g., where to add redundancy.
- Supports maintenance planning by identifying critical components.
- Spot weak links and figure out where to focus maintenance efforts.
- Helps to drive increased availability.

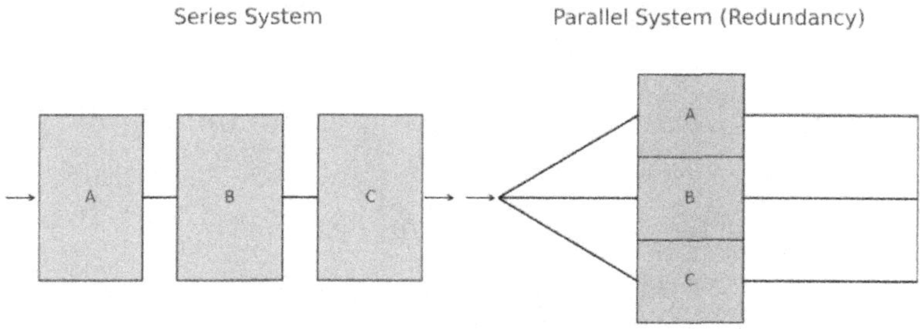

Figure 3: Reliability Block Diagram (RBD)

The whole site refinery model comprises approximately 4000 blocks (or main assets). We built it inside the Isograph Avsim Software, which is now part of Peak Avenue Isograph AWB. The study was completed in 57 days, three days ahead of schedule. The results were presented to management and area teams, highlighting which parts of the plant were contributing most to downtime and unavailability. The next step was to conduct a detailed RCM analysis on the assets contributing to unavailability losses. And so, the RCM studies started in earnest.

KPI COMPLIANCE ISN'T THE SAME AS KPI INTEGRITY

One of the first plant areas we started looking into actually surprised me. On paper, it looked like it was performing fairly well. Its Key Performance Indicators (KPIs) seemed solid, around 70% of maintenance was planned and 30% unplanned, which isn't bad. Even more impressive, it was reporting 100% compliance on planned maintenance tasks.

Yet, this area had emerged as an area of high unavailability. Something was not making sense to me. Curious, I decided to visit the workshop and have a look around for myself and to speak to a few of the area team members. I went into the planner's office and found some paper copies of planned maintenance work orders that had been completed that morning. Everything looked neat, the checkboxes were all ticked, the paper had been signed, and the planner would be closing out these work orders later that day. But something about the whole thing seemed a bit too neat. I couldn't help but notice how clean the paper was, considering the tasks involved in inspecting inclined conveyors in a rather dusty area of the plant.

That set off a few alarm bells in my head, so I decided to go out and physically retrace the steps of this particular PM task. As soon as I walked up the inclined walkway next to the conveyor, I could see a shaft wearing through the casting of a Plummer block bearing on the end of the roller. Even more concerning, there was also a rope tied around the shaft supporting it from a handrail.

Just a bit further, I noticed the gearbox coupling guard was missing, and what appeared to be a significant oil leak coming from the gearbox drive end seal. I didn't walk any further. It was obvious that no one had actually inspected this equipment properly, if at all.

However, the PM checklist had been ticked as complete, and no secondary work had been identified. That didn't sit right with me. I returned to the workshop and approached the technician whose name was on the signed work order. I asked about the PM inspection. He told me straight away that he had not done it, because he was too busy fixing high-priority failures all morning. I then asked why the sheet had been ticked and signed as complete.

He said, "Because that's what he was told to do!".

Apparently, the department had a set of strict KPI's to meet, and they consistently hit their target every week, without fail. The technician admitted that what he was doing was wrong, but he was simply following orders from the area maintenance manager. From what I could tell, there was strong competition between areas of the plant regarding performance, but the ego of this area maintenance manager was getting in the way of best practice maintenance management.

He wanted to make it appear that his area was the best-performing. Even if it meant cutting corners, faking the numbers, and being untruthful about KPIs. It was frustrating to see. This kind of behaviour completely undermines the whole point of maintenance planning and performance measurement. It also puts the reliability and safety of the plant at serious risk.

Key Performance Indicators (KPIs) are essential in maintenance and reliability because they measure how well your processes, people, and equipment are performing, and more importantly, where they're not.

Why KPIs are essential:

- Objective Measurement: KPIs turn vague feelings like "the plant seems to be running okay" into hard facts, such as "mean time between failures has dropped 20%".

- Informed Decision-Making: With clear and accurate KPIs, you know where to focus improvement efforts, whether it's improving planning, scheduling, training, or spare parts availability.

- Performance Benchmarking: KPIs allow you to track progress over time and compare performance across sites, teams, or industry standards.

- Accountability & Alignment: Everyone, from technicians to senior management, can rally around shared goals, such as reducing downtime or increasing asset availability. It creates shared purpose and transparency across the organisation.

- Proactive Culture: When teams monitor KPIs like PM compliance or backlog age, it encourages a shift from reactive firefighting to proactive planning.

Why it's crucial to be truthful with KPIs:

- False data gives a false sense of security. If you manipulate numbers just to look good, you're not solving problems, you're only hiding them. Meanwhile, the real issues get worse.

- Distorted KPIs kill improvement. If the metrics say everything is great, no one will feel urgency to change, even if the plant is barely hanging on

- Integrity builds trust. Truthful reporting builds credibility with leadership. When they trust the data, they're far more likely to help secure support for resources, tools, or changes.

- KPIs should drive action, not ego. They're not for impressing people, they're for fixing what's broken.

As the old saying goes:

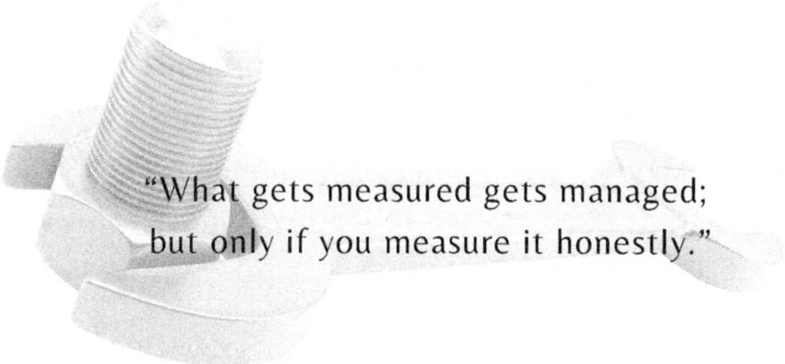

"What gets measured gets managed;
but only if you measure it honestly."

Typical KPI's in Maintenance and Reliability:

There are numerous KPIs available, but in reality, you don't need a lengthy list to manage maintenance effectively. Over the years, through trial and error and hands-on experience, I've found that just a handful of well-chosen KPIs can provide more than enough insight to drive meaningful improvements.

This list is not exhaustive, but it includes some of the key indicators I've used and trusted on my own reliability journey. I would also suggest no more than maybe six or seven KPI's are required.

Here are my top 7 KPIs (Key Performance Indicators) that offer the most insight and impact in Maintenance and Reliability. These cover performance, efficiency, cost, and culture. Once you've got those working well, you can always expand your set if needed:

1. Planned vs. Unplanned Work (%)
   - What it measures: The proportion of maintenance work that is planned ahead vs. reactive/emergency.
   - Why it matters: High levels of unplanned work lead to chaos, increased costs, and reliability issues.
     Target: >80% planned.

2. Schedule Compliance (%)
   - What it measures: The percentage of scheduled maintenance work completed within the planned timeframe.
   - Why it matters: Reflects discipline, resource alignment, and organisational reliability.
   Target: >90%.

3. Wrench Time (%)
   - What it measures: The amount of actual hands-on tool time vs. total time on the job.
   - Why it matters: Low wrench time signals inefficiency due to delays, waiting on parts, unclear instructions, etc.
   Target: 35–45% is world-class.

4. Mean Time Between Failures (MTBF)
   - What it measures: The average operating time between failures of an asset or system.
   - Why it matters: This is a direct indicator of equipment reliability.
   Improving MTBF = fewer breakdowns.

5. Mean Time to Repair (MTTR)
   - What it measures: The average time taken to diagnose and fix a system or component to restore it to full operational status.
   - Why it matters: Shorter MTTR = faster recovery, better uptime, and more agile teams.

6. Maintenance Cost as % of Replacement Asset Value (RAV)

- What it measures: Total annual maintenance cost divided by the total replacement cost of the asset base.
- Why it matters: Helps benchmark cost-effectiveness. Typical target: 2–3% for most industries.

7. RCA Cultural Indicator: % of Root Cause Analyses (RCA) Closed with Actions Completed

- What it measures: This tracks whether the organisation learns from failures and improves plant performance.
- Why it matters: It's one thing to investigate a failure, but what matters more is whether the team takes corrective action. This KPI reflects the organisation's willingness to learn from issues and prevent repeat failures.
- Use it to: Track how serious the organisation is about continuous improvement and building an authentic reliability culture.

BUILDING RELIABILITY FROM THE GROUND UP

Initially, my role at the Nickel Refinery was only meant to last six months. However, as time passed, it became clear that reliability thinking was gaining traction across the site. More and more projects were emerging, and the need for structured, strategic reliability input was being widely recognised, not just by the maintenance teams, but also by engineering, operations, and even senior leadership.

One of those projects was the new Cobalt recovery plant. Cobalt was being viewed as a valuable commodity, and the current status of the Nickel Production plant had led to Cobalt being considered a waste or by-product of the Nickel manufacturing facility. This new project was now going to recover the Cobalt.

Cobalt, as it turns out, is a highly valuable and in-demand metal used in the manufacture of Lithium-ion batteries, especially in electric vehicles (EVs), smartphones, and laptops. It plays a key role in improving energy density and extending battery life, both of which are crucial for the growing EV market and modern electronics. So suddenly, what was once waste was now seen as an opportunity and a strategic asset.

So, I was appointed as the Reliability Design Engineer on the Cobalt project. Sometimes it is also referred to as 'Design for Reliability' (DfR), and it's one of the most important (but often overlooked) parts of any reliability journey. Addressing reliability early in life ensures you can maximise asset availability and confirm the whole lifecycle of the asset. Unfortunately, reliability in many projects is often an afterthought and is only addressed during the 'Maintain' phase, frequently when it's too late. By then, many critical decisions have already been made, including layout, materials, system architecture, and equipment selection, all of which directly affect performance and maintainability. Therefore, being proactive in design can save a company millions of dollars over the lifecycle of an asset.

DESIGN FOR RELIABILITY (DFR)

Design for Reliability is a foundational element in a reliability journey because it ensures that reliability is built into assets, systems, and components that are designed to last, right from the start, rather than being attempted later through reactive maintenance or fixes. It's a structured approach to ensure that equipment meets performance targets, is easy to maintain, and delivers high availability over its entire life cycle.

Here's why DfR is so critical:

1. Prevention is Better than Cure
   - Designing for Reliability addresses potential failure modes before they become real-world problems.
   - It's far more cost-effective to prevent failures during design than to correct them during production or after deployment.

2. Reliability is Hard to Add Later
   - Once a system is built, especially in complex or mission-critical environments (e.g., aerospace, energy, infrastructure), adding reliability is expensive and often limited in effect.

- DfR ensures system architecture, materials, and processes inherently support long life and low failure rates.

3. Supports Life Cycle Cost Optimisation
   - Reliable designs reduce the total cost of ownership by minimising downtime, warranty claims, and maintenance costs over the asset's lifecycle.
   - This improves customer satisfaction and brand reputation.

4. Informs Data-Driven Decisions
   - A DfR process includes reliability modelling, FMEA, FTA, accelerated life testing, etc., to quantify and validate reliability early.
   - This enables informed decision-making across engineering, procurement, and operations.

5. Enables Cross-Functional Collaboration
   - DfR requires early and ongoing collaboration between design, reliability, quality, manufacturing, and field support teams.
   - This integration helps align performance, cost, and reliability goals from concept to delivery.

6. Speeds Up Time to Market
   - By reducing late-stage redesigns and unexpected failures in testing or early use, DfR streamlines development cycles.

Design for Reliability is really where the reliability journey begins. It lays the groundwork for everything that comes later, whether it's asset management, predictive maintenance, or lifecycle optimisation. If you get it right at the design stage, you save time, money, and a lot of future headaches.

CONFERENCE MISHAPS AND MEMORIES

Whilst allocated on the Cobalt project, I was also able to continue supporting the ARMS reliability team with their annual conference, known as Reliability Week. It was usually held in one of the major cities in Australia. Some of the venues were amazing. One of my favourites was in a hotel conference room which looked right across towards the Sydney Harbour Bridge.

I remember standing there, looking out the window and thinking how surreal it was.

Growing up in the UK, I used to see that exact bridge on TV every New Year's Eve, watching the famous fireworks show from the other side of the world. And here I was now looking across at the bridge at another reliability conference.

The Sydney Harbour Bridge really is a marvel. Did you know it took about 53,000 tons of steel to build it?

Its total length is about 3,770 feet (1,149 meters), and the top of the bridge stands 440 feet (134 meters) above the harbour. It carries eight lanes of traffic and two rail lines.

There is a cycleway for bikes and a walkway for pedestrians. It really is an iconic view in Sydney, alongside the famous 'Opera House'.

At one of the ARMS reliability conferences, I was delivering a company case study presentation, and during the morning break, I had been handed a new device – a 'presentation clicker' with a built-in laser pointer. You know the type, it plugs into your laptop and you can walk away from it and move your presentation slides forward or backwards.

I removed it from its package and went into the main conference hall; I would be up on stage soon, still nervous but safe in the knowledge that my slides had not been tampered with, as in my last experience.

The speaker before me that day was none other than my old friend from the USA, Bill Keeter. If you've ever had the chance to sit in on one of Bill's presentations or training sessions, you'll know exactly what I mean when I say he's one of the best in the business. He has a calm, steady presence and a way of delivering technical content with absolute clarity. Plus, his voice, with its deep, slow American tone, commands attention. I always enjoy listening to him.

So, there I was, sitting quietly at the back of the conference room, watching Bill in full flow, when it suddenly dawned on me that I hadn't used the new PowerPoint clicker device before. I decided to try it before heading to the stage.

So, I quietly turned on my laptop, inserted the device into my USB port and opened my presentation. Okay, this button moves the slides forward and hey presto, my slides went forward 4 slides after four clicks, slide 1... 2... 3... 4... great!

Then I tried going backwards and forwards several times. The laser light worked too. I was feeling more confident. And then... things started to get weird. My slides suddenly jumped forward without me pressing anything. So, I then clicked again and sent them backwards, then they moved forward again. I started to think this new device was taking on a life of its own.

But then, in the background, in his calm, slow, deep American tone, I heard Bill, who was on stage in the middle of his presentation, suddenly says,

"Jeez folks, I'm sorry, I really don't know what's happening to my presentation".

My stomach dropped. I pressed my clicker once more to

confirm my fear, and sure enough, Bill's presentation slides went forward one more slide. Oh no.

It turned out that Bill was using the same clicker device as I was, and I was now unknowingly controlling his slides on stage. Nobody who sat near me realised it was me, but inside, I was panicking. I quietly and quickly put my clicker down and stopped clicking, hoping the chaos would end. Bill was then able to continue. I felt terrible.

Later, I did confess to Bill and the rest of the audience that it had been me who was controlling the slide deck, and everyone burst out laughing. Thankfully, Bill, being the legend he is, also saw the funny side. Still, I felt terrible.

Now, fast forward a few years to 2023. I was presenting at a Noria conference in Florida and preparing on stage to present a paper when I spotted Bill walking into the presentation room. He waved and, with a cheeky grin, held up in his hand a 'presentation clicker'. We both laughed.

Surely, he wasn't going to get his own back on me now, all these years later. He didn't, but he did keep me wondering throughout the presentation.

Nice one, Bill!

MY PROUDEST MOMENT

Life in Townsville was going really well, and I had been onsite at the Nickel refinery now for almost a year. I was enjoying everything the tropical north Queensland, sunshine, palm trees, and that laid-back Aussie vibe. We had a steady stream of friends and family visiting us from overseas, and it was always a joy to show them around.

Then, one ordinary evening after dinner, everything changed.

My wife turned to me and said she thought she might be pregnant. She was calm, but I could tell there was a mix of excitement and nerves in her voice. The next day, she took a test, and just like that, the result we had been hoping for was staring back at us.

We were going to have a baby.

It's hard to put into words how I felt in that moment. Happy? Absolutely. Scared? A little. But more than anything, I felt this deep, grounding sense of joy and purpose.

And then in October 2005, that joy reached a whole new level. I became the happiest man on the planet. Our beautiful son, Connor, came into the world.

Becoming a dad for the first time is like unlocking a part of your heart you didn't even know existed, a strange, beautiful combination of awe, fear, pride, and pure, overwhelming love.

In an instant, your world shifts. I know people say that all the time, but it really does. That tiny, squirming human in your arms, who looks vaguely like a potato and somehow exactly like you, now becomes the centre of your universe. You're not just a man anymore; you're Dad. That single word, just three letters, now carries a lifetime of meaning.

It still is and will always be my proudest moment in my life.

Becoming a father reshaped how I measured success. Suddenly, achievements weren't only tied to career milestones, but also to the love, responsibility, and perspective that family brought. That shift made me see my time in Townsville differently, not just as a professional growth opportunity, but also as a personal transformation.

Looking back, Townsville gave me more than just experience with block diagrams, KPIs, and design-for-reliability projects. It gave me stories that would stay with me for life: the pride of presenting at international conferences, the laughter of accidentally controlling a friend's slides on stage, the quiet awe of holding my son for the first time.

These moments blurred the lines between career and life, reminding me that growth happens not only in boardrooms or workshops, but also in friendships, in family, and in the courage to live fully wherever you are planted. However, after several more months in Townsville and pushing Connor up and down the Strand in his pram, we decided the tropical heat in Queensland was becoming unbearable.

The truth is, as much as we loved the lifestyle and the people, we just never fully adapted to living in such humid, sweaty conditions. After several lengthy discussions (and many sweaty days), we decided it was time for a change. So, I spoke with the ARMS management, and we all agreed that a move back to Victoria would be the best option for both work and family. So that's what we did.

After two incredible years, we bid our farewells to the north, packed up our belongings (with a few tears and a lot of baby gear), and headed to the state of Victoria, where we continued our Aussie Adventure.

What began as a temporary assignment had become something far greater: the foundation for adventures and opportunities that would stretch far beyond Australia's shores, shaping both my career and my life in ways I could never have imagined.

Chapter 8

Growing, Living & Letting Go

Growing, Living & Letting Go

"The magic in new beginnings is truly the
most powerful of them all,"
Josiyah Martin.

Our time in Australia had turned into something far bigger than we'd ever imagined. What started as a career opportunity soon became a rich, life-changing experience filled with new friendships, exciting travel, professional growth, and the kind of moments that shape you forever. I found myself working across a wide range of industries, gaining valuable experience and leading complex investigations, not just in Australia but around the world.

Each new site, each challenge, added another layer to my understanding of reliability, leadership, and people.

At the same time, life at home was evolving too. Sharon and I were learning what it meant to raise a young family so far from our own families. We had built a strong network of friends in the village of Barwon Heads, some of whom were even from my hometown of Clitheroe, and that gave us a real sense of belonging. But as time went on, I started to see things more clearly through Sharon's eyes.

This chapter isn't just about leaving; it's about living. It's about finding your place in the world, then realising that where you belong might not always be where you stay. And sometimes, growth isn't just about reaching new heights; it's also about knowing when to make tough decisions.

FACILITATING CHANGE, NOT JUST FIXES

My work travels around Australia continued to take me to some fascinating places and different industries. Whether it was working with teams in the rail sector, food processing plants, chocolate factories, oil refineries, or dairy production facilities, each experience brought something new.

Supporting such a wide range of industries gave me exposure to different challenges, technologies, and ways of working and that variety turned out to be one of the most valuable parts of my journey. Every site had its own unique set of assets, and the RCM studies on such a wide and varied asset base were adding to my personal growth as a Reliability Engineer.

Along with the reliability studies, the Root Cause Analysis facilitations that I led on some high-impact failures and incidents were such an amazing experience, not just in Australia, but globally. Being trusted to lead those investigations was a humbling and rewarding experience.

Each time, I was learning and improving my own facilitation skill set, including how to ask better questions, guide diverse groups, manage strong opinions, and bring people together to find effective and practical solutions. (See Table 2 below.) It's incredible to look back and see how far I've come since the very first Apollo RCA in New Zealand. And certainly, so much further than those early days trying to navigate successful outcomes in ICI with 5 Whys and Fishbone, it really puts the journey into perspective.

Country	Problem	Department
NZ	Premature Valve Failures	Reliability
Australia	Light Curtain Trip ($1.1 million saving)	Production
Australia	Accident – High Potential Near Miss	Safety
UK	Calciner Seal Issues (£550k saving)	Reliability
UK	Offshore Firewater Pump Failure	Safety
Switzerland	Construction Site Fatality	Safety
USA	Oil Storage Tank Seal Failure	Environmental
Ireland	Conveyor Fire	Safety
Ireland	Bio Safety Cabinet Test Failure	Quality
Poland	Project Over-Run	Production
USA	Plant Shutdown due to Emissions	Environmental
UK	Offshore Platform – High Potential Near Miss	Safety

Table 2: Global Incident Investigation Facilitations

One of the more unforgettable incidents I was involved in happened at a remote coal mine in the rural outback of Australia. I was flown in urgently after a serious event had brought the entire site to a standstill.

A Ute (what folks in the UK might call a pickup truck) had been reversed over; yes, reversed over by one of those massive Cat797 Dump Trucks in the early hours of the morning, around 2 a.m. When I arrived at the site, the mine manager didn't mince his words. He said, 'Enough was enough.' The site had experienced far too many near misses, and if the safety record continued like this, it was only a matter of time before it led to a fatality. Years earlier, the same mine had been the site of one of Australia's worst mining disasters. That tragic legacy still hung in the air, and safety was a top priority.

At the time of the incident, the mine was operating at full capacity. Production demands were sky-high, and in response, the site was bringing in new staff as fast as possible. New operators were being trained and fast-tracked to operate mine equipment quickly; maybe too quickly.

Previously, new staff training assessments were managed during the day shift only; however, to keep up with demand, they are now being performed 24 hours a day. That decision played a key role in what unfolded. This particular incident occurred in the early hours of the morning. A training assessor was performing an assessment of a new driver who was being assessed, removing a 360 digger from the back of a low loader located in the mine. When the assessor arrived in the Ute, the 360 digger was isolated with a 'do not start' tag on the starter.

The new driver waited in the digger for news from maintenance before going ahead with the manoeuvre.

The assessor sat in his Ute waiting for news from maintenance. Conversations were being recorded through various channels, including the operator and maintenance channels. The assessor was completing training paperwork inside the Ute, with the engine running, lights and air conditioning on inside the Ute. Whilst completing the paperwork, the assessor heard a reversing bleeper and immediately looked up, only to see the large rear wheel and tyre of a dump truck approaching his vehicle. With seconds to react, he shifted the Ute into gear and accelerated just as the dump truck reversed over it. The rest of the Ute was crushed to the ground.

Miraculously, the Ute driver survived. When I say those dump trucks are enormous, I mean they are truly massive. It's hard to imagine something like that happening and someone walking away from it, but somehow, the driver got out with just a few scratches.

It was a close call; far too close!

I also delivered some Apollo RCA training to a group of military personnel in Brisbane. They had joined one of our public training sessions, and I remember clearly that on the very first day, their team leader pulled me aside and asked,

"Will you be covering any helicopter incidents as part of the training?" I was taken aback.

"No," I said, "we don't have any helicopter-related exercises planned. Why do you ask?"

It turned out that the team he had brought along to the training was a maintenance crew that had performed some maintenance work on a Royal Australian Navy Sea King helicopter. The same helicopter had tragically dropped out of the sky and crashed on the island of Nias whilst on a humanitarian mission following an earthquake in the region. Of the 11 military personnel on board, nine were killed in the accident. It was a devastating loss.

Later, a formal investigation into the crash found that the main reason for the accident was that a nut and a split pin in the helicopter's flight controls were incorrectly fitted. Even more concerning, the report highlighted that the squadron responsible for the helicopter's maintenance routinely took shortcuts. The final findings came with a staggering 256 recommendations.

That number alone tells you just how deep the systemic issues ran.

During a break in the training, the maintenance supervisor came and spoke with me, one-to-one, and he opened up about the incident. You could see the weight he was carrying; it was written all over his face. He told me how intense the pressure had been since the crash, both personally and professionally.

He was married with a young family. I could tell this poor guy was suffering as a result of the incident and the blame being put on his shoulders and those of his team.

That conversation has stuck with me all these years. I still think about him from time to time, wondering how he's doing, hoping he has found peace and support to work through that trauma. It's hard to describe, but there was something incredibly human about that moment, something that reminded me how these technical failures we investigate are often deeply personal for those involved.

There is a perception in the military, with incidents like this, that you are deemed guilty until you can prove you are innocent. It's a mindset shaped by the rigid structure and culture within the military justice system. That's why it was so encouraging when, after completing the Apollo RCA training, the team decided to perform an internal Apollo RCA investigation on the incident. The Apollo method promotes a 'no blame' approach. It is crucial to focus on condition-based causes rather than just the actions of individuals.

That's always been something I've believed in strongly. When you focus on conditional causes, systemic, environmental, and procedural, you get far better solutions than when you limit the investigation to individual actions alone.

As Dean Gano, the founder of Apollo RCA, often said,

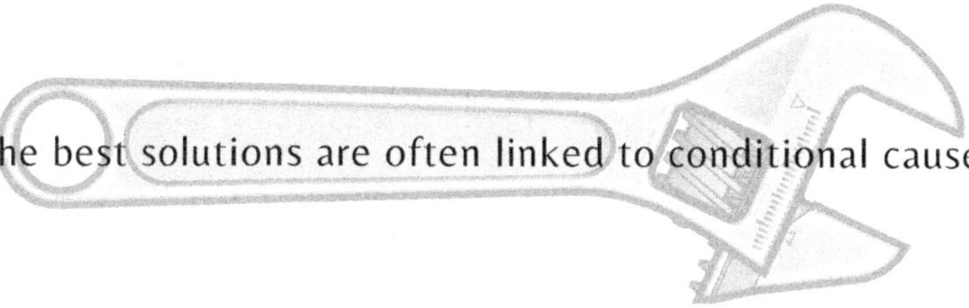

"The best solutions are often linked to conditional causes."

That philosophy aligns closely with my own experience over the years. It's not about avoiding accountability; it's about solving the real problem so it doesn't happen again.

BLAME STOPS LEARNING

I also remember meeting Professor Andrew Hopkins at a safety event in Australia. He was the author of the book 'The Longford Disaster' and was also an expert witness at the royal commission that followed the incident at the Longford Esso plant near Melbourne.

The accident occurred on 25 September 1998, when a pressure vessel at the plant suddenly ruptured. This caused a serious jet fire that quickly spread, engulfing a large part of the facility. The fires burned intensely for two days before emergency crews managed to get them under control.

Sadly, two workers lost their lives, and eight others were severely injured. The incident also caused a massive disruption to Victoria's gas supply, affecting homes, businesses, and hospitals across the state.

Esso initially blamed the accident on the negligence of plant operators. They even produced training records from one particular operator as evidence to show that this person should have been able to deal with the plant problem and prevent it from escalating. The findings of the Longford Royal Commission, however, focused on Esso's safety practices rather than on actions by individual operators:

"The causes of the accident on 25 September 1998 amounted to a failure to provide and maintain, so far as practicable, a safe working environment without health risks. This constituted a breach or breaches of section 21 of the [Victorian] Occupational Health and Safety Act 1985."

Everywhere you look, when something goes wrong, there is 'Blame'. It's almost instinctive. Please watch your news channel this evening, and you'll see what I mean. Politicians are the worst for it, always blaming, blaming, blaming. However, the problem is that when we focus on blame, we stop learning. As I mentioned in Chapter 3, we stop addressing the actual issues.

Blame is a barrier to genuine problem-solving, yet it appears everywhere: in government, business, healthcare, and even our personal lives. Pointing fingers may feel satisfying in the moment, but it leaves the root cause unaddressed, ensuring the same issue will surface again.

That's why I have tried several times to get UK politicians to look at the Apollo method of RCA. It's a structured, logical approach to understanding the real causes behind problems, without the need to blame individuals.

It helps people uncover the real reasons behind failures, and more importantly, it provides them with a way forward. Sadly, I haven't had much luck. I honestly believe they need something like this, desperately.

However, the reality is that the blame game still works for them. It keeps the spotlight away from themselves, perhaps!

I even offered my local NHS Trust some free facilitation time to explore why they continued to overspend on their annual budgets. This wasn't about calling anyone out; it was about helping them improve. I made that offer through my local MP at the time, but for whatever reason, it was turned down.

It's frustrating, to be honest. There's a huge opportunity to shift our mindset from blame to learning, but many parts of the system seem stuck in old ways. Maybe, one day, the culture may shift. I really hope it does.

Because the sooner we let go of blame, the sooner we'll start solving real problems.

A DETOUR IN PAPUA NEW GUINEA

On a more positive and fascinating note, one of the more memorable experiences in my career came while I was based in Australia. I had the chance to travel across to Papua New Guinea, to the OK Tedi mine, to deliver a series of reliability training courses. Now, this wasn't your average site visit.

OK Tedi was a huge copper mine tucked away high in the mountains, and getting there was an adventure in itself. I flew in on a small plane from Cairns, Australia, landing on a dusty airstrip surrounded by dense forest and mountain peaks. Once there, I stayed in a simple mine camp; my own little cabin with a bed, a toilet, and a very noisy air conditioning unit stuck on the wall. Basic, but enough.

At night, I had to sleep under a mosquito net I brought with me, something I was very thankful for. Mosquitoes don't take holidays in PNG! The reliability training was going well, and as the site was just starting out on its reliability journey, there was a real appetite to learn. I met quite a few expats who were permanently based at the camp.

Interestingly, copper wasn't the only thing coming out of the OK Tedi mine; gold was also a byproduct at this time. Quite often, a bit of it got washed down the OK Tedi River, which meant many of the locals were busy panning for gold as a source of income.

The mine even had its own convenience store and a goldsmith who was employed to take gold that was found by the mine itself, not the locals and turn it into jewellery.

Now, I know what you are thinking!

Every time you left the site, you were searched. If you had any gold in your possession, you needed to always have a receipt to prove you'd bought it through the approved channels. Otherwise, it was confiscated. Every evening while sitting in my cabin, I'd get a gentle knock on the door from a local trying to sell me gold, often at a very cheap price. And while I understood that making the sale could really help their family, I was strictly forbidden from making the purchase. No exceptions. It was a strange mix of opportunity and restriction.

I was given meal vouchers to get my meals in the site canteen. I wasn't sure what to expect, but it turned out to be an interesting dining experience. You would queue up like we used to when getting school dinners, and you would choose what food you wanted on your plate. The food was more than reasonable, much better than I expected. But what really surprised me was how the locals ate their meals.

They would pile their plate with food very high. What shocked me the most was that they would add the main course and dessert on the same plate.

You'd see someone with a meat chop sitting right next to a sponge cake and custard, all on the same plate! That combination really turned my stomach. Anyway, I got my first meal at the site, handed over my voucher, and when I turned round, I wasn't exactly sure where to sit. The canteen was busy, and I noticed I was the only white guy. I wasn't sure if there was some kind of seating etiquette that I should follow, or if I might be intruding by sitting at the wrong table. I felt a little awkward, to be honest.

There was one completely empty table, so I went over and sat by myself. Bit by bit, I noticed people coming over and taking the chairs away from my table; the locals chose to sit at other tables that were already overcrowded. It was uncomfortable. I started wondering why nobody would sit with me. I couldn't shake the uneasy feeling.

The following day, I spoke with the expat manager, Martin, and I told him what had happened and how I felt. He laughed and said,

"Oh my, just sit anywhere! And once they know where I am from, they will want to talk about English football."

And you know what? He was absolutely right. The following evening, I decided to try again. This time, I walked confidently into the canteen and sat down right in the middle of approximately 20 locals.

I introduced myself as 'Gary from England', and just like that, their faces lit up. They immediately started talking about English football nonstop. Someone had even heard of Blackburn Rovers, which made me smile. I was honestly relieved!

From that point on, everything changed. They were such a friendly bunch, full of energy and curiosity. It didn't take long for me to feel like part of the group. What a great set of people, I really enjoyed my time at OK Tedi.

One of the team members on the reliability training course at OK Tedi was a local Papua New Guinea engineer called Gibert Hamambi. I am so proud to say I have watched Gilbert excel and rise through the ranks on his own personal Reliability Journey. He also wrote a book and has many followers on LinkedIn. I've kept in contact with Gilbert, and I recently just missed catching up with him in Singapore by a matter of hours! He's one of our well-known global Reliability superstars. He certainly understood the value of Reliability and was able to support embedding the right culture to drive Reliability forward at OK Tedi. Top man Gilbert!!

During the trip, some expats, including Martin, planned a hike to a nearby mountain called Mount Robinson, and I was invited along on this trek. Now, I was initially hesitant as I hadn't really brought any of my trekking clothing or equipment. I was assured that my footwear was suitable and that I would be given a small rucksack containing water and food. With that, I thought, why not?

So, Sunday morning rolled around, and we all piled into vehicles and drove off. We parked near the entrance to the mine, leaving our vehicles at the security hut. We started off on a narrow path that ran alongside a tall, grassy field. I still don't know what kind of grass it was; maybe it was sugar cane. All I knew was that it towered over me like some kind of leafy skyscraper.

We then reached the path at the base of the mountain that would take us up Mount Robinson and onwards to the summit. I call it a path; it was not really marked out, but more like scrambling over roots, ducking under branches, and brushing off low-hanging spiderwebs.

The rain from the day before had left everything slick and muddy. That's when I started thinking: maybe my shoes weren't as "suitable" as everyone thought. Still, the company was good. Everyone was friendly, chatting away, making me feel included despite my lack of gear and experience. I continued with the trek. It was humid, and I was sweating. As we climbed higher, before long, I was starting to feel unwell. I started slowing down, feeling lightheaded and dizzy. A headache crept in, and I never get headaches.

That's when I knew something wasn't right. I stopped for water and to catch my breath, hoping it would pass. It didn't. Nausea joined the party. I hated to admit it, but I knew I was slowing the group down.

I alerted them to my condition and made a decision to turn around and return to the cars next to the security hut. They were all incredibly supportive. I was starting with altitude sickness, whilst I knew I was in the mountains, I had not appreciated what the altitude of the OK Tedi mine site was (approximately 2000m). Some of the team offered to come back with me, but I insisted they continue.

"I will follow my steps back down the mountain and head to the security hut," I said confidently. "I'll be fine." What could possibly go wrong? Well...

I started my descent and was manoeuvring in and out of the trees and under low branches, avoiding the spiders' webs. I eventually made it to the sugar cane field. Perfect, I thought. Just follow the path back to the security hut. Simple.

Except that the path I had walked along was missing.

Completely vanished!

I stood there for a moment in disbelief.

"How was that possible?" I thought; my hand on my head.

I spun around, scanning the area. No path. Just an endless stretch of towering grass. I was expecting to reach the path, turn left, and follow it back to the security hut. But now... I had no idea where I was.

This is the part where I'd love to tell you I used some kind of survival instinct. That I looked at the position of the sun, made a compass out of a leaf and a needle, and confidently set off like Bear Grylls. But no. I was just a confused, sweating guy in the middle of nowhere, completely and utterly lost.

I thought, if I kept the mountain on my left and headed left, I'd eventually stumble back to the hut. However, this meant going into the sugarcane fields. Tall, dense, and possibly home to... well, who knows what? Snakes? Wild boars? Tigers? Do they even have tigers in Papua New Guinea? I should have done my research. Still, I had no choice.

I pulled back the sugar cane and stepped into the dense vegetation like Tarzan in the movies. Moving slowly one step at a time, trying not to panic. While walking, another thought occurred to me. I had read a little about life in Papua New Guinea, and what was concerning was that some tribes had only stopped cannibalism in the 1950s when Australia took over the rule in the country.

Was that real? Was it just some sensationalist nonsense? Either way, it didn't help my nerves.

I knew I was moving in the right direction, but I felt like I was far away from the path I had initially taken. Here I was standing in the middle of a sugar cane field in Papua New Guinea, no phone, no survival bag, no survival book, just me, on my own and the buzzing insects. And as I stood there, surrounded by walls of sugar cane, I couldn't help wondering how the hell I ended up here. Sharon is going to kill me if I don't get home.

I was also feeling slightly better after descending from the mountain. The headache had eased, and the nausea had faded, thankfully. But now a new kind of anxiety had set in. I was lost. Well and truly lost, deep in a sugar cane field in Papua New Guinea, wearing a shirt that now reeked of sweat and desperation. My clothes practically screamed,

"This guy definitely isn't from around here."

I'd been stumbling through the cane for what felt like an eternity, probably just over an hour, but when you're lost in unfamiliar terrain, time doesn't tick normally. It stretches. I was bushwhacking my way through the thick green stalks like it was a corn maze designed by Mother Nature after a bad breakup, full of spite, humidity, and absolutely no sense of direction.

Then it happened.

Suddenly, I heard it - crack! Rustle! Crack! Rustle!

I froze. "What the hell is that noise?" I stopped breathing, and I could see ahead of me the sugar cane moving from side to side, as if something was pushing through them.

Something big.

Was it a wild animal? A lion? A tiger, maybe?

Wait. Did they have lions and tigers here? I don't know, but I am about to find out! Possibly the hard way.

This was like a scene straight out of a Stephen King Novel. I was terrified.

Then, out they came.

Suddenly, two local tribesmen and a young tribal boy appear through the tall cane. They were dressed in traditional attire, which is to say, not much, and the young boy was holding a rather large, very real machete. I stood there, frozen to the spot, my mouth dry, my brain firing off every emergency signal it could muster. And I thought to myself: Well... this is how National Geographic ends.

I wanted to run, but I couldn't. I was too scared to move. I was literally frozen to the spot. One of the elders squints at me, not aggressively, more like he's trying to figure out if I'm a lost tourist or an exceptionally confused bird. I stayed calm, nodded, smiled and waved with a small, friendly gesture. I wanted to say 'live long and prosper', made famous by Captain Spock of Star Trek. It was a well-known greeting and symbol of goodwill. But I guessed they had never watched Star Trek; they wouldn't understand.

They stared. I stared. Time slowed to a crawl.

Then I suddenly remembered reading about the cannibalism, what if these two tribesmen didn't know it had been stopped in the 1950s, what if I was next on the menu?

They speak Pidgin to me, and all I can say is, "I'm lost and need help." But they didn't understand, I could have been saying "I am a chicken and I respect your canoe." – I know the English language is one of the most common globally used languages in the world, but it hadn't yet made it to this sugar cane field in the remote mountains of Papua New Guinea and I wasn't in the mood to start teaching English.

They just kept staring at me.

Then, suddenly, one of the tribesmen slaps his thigh, and the other does an exaggerated impression of me flailing through the sugarcane like a broken wind-up toy. I must've looked ridiculous. They clearly thought I was the funniest thing they've seen since a wild pig ran off with someone's wedding cake. Eventually, they passed by me, still laughing, and continued on their way, machetes in hand, no doubt with a great story to tell back at their village. Fortunately, they seemed more interested in getting back than turning me into dinner that evening.

So off I went, stumbling forward again like some off-brand Bear Grylls who had lost his film crew and his dignity. Honestly, congratulations, Gary, you've just navigated a near-death experience and a full-blown cultural misfire, all before evening dinner. Phew.

Finally! Finally, I saw it. The security hut. That glorious little building had never looked so beautiful. I almost cried. I don't think I've ever felt so relieved in my life. The local security team saw me approaching, bedraggled and wild-eyed, and kindly allowed me to rest in their hut until the walking expat crew returned.

It was great to see the team of expats return to the hut a few hours later. And boy, did I have a story to tell them. The story became a legend at the mine site for a while:

'The English engineer, who found himself lost while out on a walk.'

WHERE PROCESS MEETS PEOPLE

But back to working in Australia, things really started to shift for me professionally. I had begun to support the Australian Aluminium Smelting industry, and before long, I became an accidental Subject Matter Expert (SME) in this industry. Looking back, the two years working at the Nickel Refinery certainly paved the way for my progression into the Aluminium industry.

In addition to providing reliability support, I was soon approached by the Health and Safety group to assist with incident investigations. One particular site was experiencing a high number of near misses and minor accidents. I was asked to review their investigation approach to these incidents.

That's when I realised that all incidents, regardless of severity, were being investigated with the same tool, the 5 Whys approach. On paper, 5 Whys is deceptively simple. Ask "why" five times, and voilà, you've reached the root cause. Right?

Not quite!

Further review of the individual reports displayed a lack of understanding and inconsistency in the approach and use of 5 Whys.

Some investigations already had a problem and solution written down, but without asking why it happened. Others started from the end and looked back, while some started from the beginning and moved forward. Overall, the quality was very mixed.

I compiled my findings and sat down with the management team to share my concerns.

"Has the team actually been trained in Root Cause Analysis (RCA)?" I asked. "Specifically, have they been taught how to effectively apply the 5 Whys process currently being used?"

Their response floored me. "Gary, seriously, do you think we need to train people to ask why 5 five times? That approach is simple. Ask why 5 times and identify the root cause".

At this point, I had to hold back a chuckle. I then gently, but firmly, pointed out some of the failings I had identified. They had no business process, no site champion and no quality assurance reviews of the investigation; they were just a tick box exercise to say the review had been "completed" but not understood. I explained that if the company continued on the current path with incident investigations, then at some stage, a fatality was going to happen.

To their credit, the leadership took my concerns seriously

and what followed was a pivotal moment for the site.

They agreed that improvements could be made and committed to a site-wide improvement initiative. We roll out a structured review and training of key facilitators in using the Apollo RCA methodology.

Another memorable investigation activity took place during a high-stakes annual shutdown at an Oil Refinery. The operation involved a critical piece of equipment, a tube-and-shell type heat exchanger.

The shutdown was meticulously planned, and this exchanger sat firmly on the project's critical path. A new tube bundle, with a special design, approximately 10 meters long and fabricated from a precious metal due to the process demands, had been manufactured and shipped from Malaysia. Everything was teed up. The site had contractors ready to install it. Due to its length, the installation was going to be a delicate operation. It was part of the annual shutdowns' critical path. Hence, they could not afford any problems; the shutdown timeline was based on having this exchanger operational as soon as possible.

Everything was going well. The rigging and lifting operations were well-coordinated. Inch by inch, the bundle moved into position. The finish line was just approximately one metre from being in its home position.

And then, it happened.

The tube bundle caught the edge of the tube body. It wasn't aligned in the correct position. But rather than stop, reassess, and realign, someone made the fateful decision to keep pushing forward into the final home position.

That's when the tubes were ripped open like a tin opener opening a can. Imagine the sound. The precious tubes tore open, ripped, sheared, ruined. The operation came to a screeching halt. The bundle was damaged beyond repair.

Inspections and photographs were taken. Then came the blame. Lots of it. This is when a decision was made to bring in an external facilitator to perform a root cause analysis of the incident. And that was me. I had the pleasure of leading this investigation. When I arrived at the site and got to the room, I knew right away that I had too many people in there. I had 10 contractors, 10 ACME company staff and a senior manager from both ACME and the contracting company sat in the room.

We began by agreeing on the problem definition. That was the easy part. But then, when asked for some of the possible causes, everybody remained quiet. I asked a few more times by rewording the question, but still I got silence. Nobody was prepared to speak out due to fear of being blamed. The senior managers, sitting at the back with arms crossed and eyebrows raised, had created an invisible gag order. I could see it in every hesitant glance and shallow breath. So, I paused the session and invited the group for a coffee break. On the way out, I asked the managers to remain out of the room when we reconvened. They were reluctant, but it was obvious to me that they were the reason nobody was talking.

We returned to the room without the managers, and then it all erupted. The room exploded. Frustration, blame, and anger all came pouring out. Fingers pointed in every direction. It was loud, raw, and emotional.

As a facilitator, these moments test you. You have to manage the group; you have to protect people from abuse.

So, I called a time-out again to reset the room and reestablish some ground rules. I explained we were here to understand what went wrong and, more importantly, how to make sure it never happened again. Eventually, we reached a breakthrough. The investigation was ultimately concluded with 'no blame' being apportioned to either party and some clear solutions to prevent this type of incident from happening again in the future.

But this was a tough investigation, mainly due to the size of the team put forward for the investigation and the strong characters from within, trying to derail the process and use 'blame' as the solution.

The size of a team in an RCA facilitation is essential. If the team is too small, it may lack the necessary expertise, critical information, or frontline experience, which could be missed. If the team is too large (as was the case here), then many people want to be heard, side conversations start taking place, and hierarchical influence can limit open discussion. I always say,

"More people don't always mean better answers – just more noise."

Having the right size team. I've found that a sweet spot is typically between 4 and 8 people. This enables active engagement from the entire team, ensuring a cross-functional mix of the right people, depending on the event being investigated.

TASMANIA

On a lighter note, when I wasn't knee-deep in RCA investigations or shutdown schedules, I did make time to explore. One area I enjoyed visiting in Australia was Tasmania. It is like Australia's quirky little sibling, smaller, cooler and full of surprises. You can drive for an hour and hit every kind of weather and still arrive at a bakery that's somehow won 'Australia's Best Pie' three years in a row. A place I always recommend to people who visit Tasmania is a location called Port Arthur, about 90 minutes from Hobart.

It is one of Australia's most fascinating and most hauntingly beautiful historical sites, steeped in convict-era history, surrounded by dramatic coastline, and home to stories that both chill and inspire. Port Arthur was established in 1830. It served as a penal colony for Britain's worst convicts, those who reoffended after arriving in Australia. It was designed to reform them through hard labour, discipline, and isolation.

Today, it stands as a haunting open-air museum and a UNESCO World Heritage site, and I can say with confidence that if you ever find yourself in Tasmania, it's well worth visiting. Bring good walking shoes and a healthy curiosity. You'll need both.

Now, here's a fun bit of cultural trivia I picked up during my time in Australia. The English in Australia are often referred to as Poms or Pommys, which I was told was short for P.O.M.E., supposedly standing for 'Prisoner of Mother England'. True or not, it makes for a good story over a beer.
Historically, in Australia, saying you had convict blood in your lineage was a source of embarrassment. Families would go to great lengths to hide the fact that their Great Great Grandad was a thief who stole a loaf of bread and got deported. But now, well, it's trendy. You can hear Australians nowadays comparing their genealogy as if it were a competitive sport.

"Mine stole a cow and punched a magistrate – what did yours do?"

It's almost like a reverse class system. If your ancestor was a free settler, well, that's boring, but if they arrived in chains, survived scurvy and built a homestead with a teaspoon, then you're a legend! Honestly, I enjoyed that kind of cultural twist.

THE RELIABILITY OF THE EVERYDAY

While visiting Tasmania, the main customer was an old zinc smelter; it was an interesting old factory and known as the world's third oldest zinc refinery, commencing operations in 1916. Walking around that site felt like time travel, thick with the scent of metal and machinery, echoing with the hum of processes that had evolved over a century.

It was also the first time I had come across alcohol breath testing machines in the car park. The policy was straightforward.

If you had been out the night before and turned up for work under the influence of alcohol, this was an instant dismissal. But the company, in what I'd say was both challenging and fair. To give you a chance, the company has installed breath test machines in the car park. If you fail the car park test, you will not be allowed to enter the site.

But once you passed through the gate? They had lights on the barrier; if the light flashed on entry, you were officially tested as part of the 'random' selection process. If you failed the test, you would be dismissed. They also had random drug testing in place.

I facilitated an excellent Failure Modes Effects Criticality Analysis (FMECA) here on a large and very old asset, which was mainly mechanical in nature with very few modern automation items installed. That was what we call a single point of failure. When the asset failed, production stopped. The FMECA study took nearly 3 weeks to complete. By the end, we had identified a jaw-dropping 1798 failure modes. Each failure mode is capable of stopping the production line.

Among them, the highest impact failure mode stood out like a flare in the night: "Light Curtain Trip."

Now, this wasn't even an old failure mode; it was associated with a new device installed just 18 months earlier. What was interesting here was that it was only picked up through discussions with the Operations team; the Engineers dismissed the problem, claiming the device was working as designed. When we quantified the losses in terms of production loss, it resulted in financial losses of $1 million per year.

Nobody could say why this trip was occurring so frequently,

at least once per shift, or what was causing it. At that point, we decided to carry out an Apollo RCA on that single failure mode. The RCA lasted 4 hours. In that time, 62 causes and 11 root causes were identified. With the solutions implemented following the RCA investigation, the problem was eliminated, and higher production levels were recognised.

The most valuable lessons I took from this study were the strong link between RCM and RCA. But also, the importance of communicating with the operations teams. When we are discussing failure modes, they may not be just mechanical or electrical items; we could also have some operational issues that need to be addressed. That's why listening to our plant operators is absolutely crucial.

Whether you're producing chocolate, bottling beer, or drilling for oil, one truth holds across all industries: the frontline operators are your first line of defence. These individuals are in the thick of it every single day. They are the eyes and ears of your production facility, and they're often the first to detect early signs of trouble.

For instance, an operator notices a small issue; the machine only stops once per shift, for just a minute, before hitting the reset button. It's not dramatic, and everything continues to run smoothly. But the fact that the machine restarts doesn't mean the underlying issue has gone away.

These kinds of "high-frequency, short-duration" events are easy to dismiss. At first, they seem harmless. After all, production continues, right?

But over time, several concerning behaviours start to emerge:

- Operators stop reporting faults, believing nothing will be done about them.
- They begin to develop workarounds, tweaks and tricks to get the job done, without going through any formal safety checks or risk assessments. These workarounds quietly become the new "normal" and are typically only uncovered after a severe failure occurs... when it's already too late.

Sound familiar?

This is where Reliability starts to break down: one minor, ignored issue at a time. Just like safety, Reliability hinges on the small things. Ignore the minor symptoms, and eventually, you'll be facing a major failure.

During Reliability Studies or RCA (Root Cause Analysis) sessions, we often hear familiar comments from operators:

- "We've been doing it that way for years."
- "We kept reporting it, but nothing ever changed."
- "That task used to be on our checklist, but we dropped it because it never found anything."

Let me give you one striking example: an operator regularly performed torque checks on a rotating asset at the end of each shift. The task was removed because it seemed unnecessary. Fast forward two years and, surprise! A reliability investigation into repeated breakdowns revealed that sheared bolts were the top failure mode. The torque checks were reinstated, and the failures stopped.

The lesson? Sometimes the simplest routines prevent the biggest headaches.

And speaking of surprises, let me share a personal story, one that had nothing to do with a factory floor but everything to do with awareness and luck. I had just landed in Tasmania for a work trip, after picking up my hire car at the airport and drove to Hobart to my hotel for the next few days. I parked on the street just up from the hotel as they did not have an official car park. As I left the car and walked down to the hotel, I heard an almighty loud crash. I turned around only to see the back of my hire car all crumpled with another vehicle stuck in the back end of it! I couldn't quite believe what I was seeing. I had been sitting in that vehicle seconds earlier.

Instinctively, I ran back to check if the driver of the other vehicle was okay, but to my surprise, there was no driver... and driverless cars were not yet on the road, unless Tasmania was testing some secret prototypes.

It turned out the car had been left on at the top of the hill by the vehicle's owner without the handbrake on. After they left their vehicle, it started to move slowly at first, but then it picked up speed until it used my rental car as a stopping point. I had only had the car for 40 minutes, and now it was a write-off! Luckily, nobody was injured. But the whole situation could have been so much worse.

That moment reminded me just how easily preventable incidents can be if we pay attention to the small things. Just like that missing handbrake, ignoring minor operational issues at a plant might not cause immediate chaos, but eventually, it will. And the consequences can be serious.

THE HARDEST GOODBYES COME WITH THE WARMEST MEMORIES

Life continued in the state of Victoria. Work meant I was often away, travelling regularly, leaving Sharon and Connor at home. We had a great group of friends and even quite a few people from my hometown of Clitheroe living in the village of Barwon Heads.

Having a solid support network made life a little easier. There was something comforting about that, familiar accents, shared memories, and the kind of friendships that start to feel like family. Because really, when you live so far from your home base, your friends do become your family.

But even in the midst of all that: sunshine, beach walks, and friendly faces, I knew Sharon was struggling. She missed home. She was homesick, and now with Connor in her arms, the need for family was much stronger. She needed the comfort of knowing someone else could hold the baby while she made a cup of tea. That kind of thing.

One evening, we got a babysitter, a rare treat and the two of us went out for a dinner date. Since Connor was born, it had always been the three of us, with little time spent as a couple. But that night, we sat across from each other, with a lovely meal, a nice bottle of wine, and a bit of space to breathe. We chatted and discussed our situation in Australia, and of course, homesickness came up; it always did. I could tell Sharon had been holding in a lot.

And then, somewhere between dessert and the last glass of wine, I asked the million-dollar question, "Would you like to go back home?"
She didn't hesitate. "Yes", she said.

Just one word. But it said everything.

My stomach twisted into a knot. I won't lie. I'd never been happier anywhere in my life than I was in Australia. For me, this place was home. I'd fallen in love with it; the people, the lifestyle, even the smell of the ocean on an early morning walk.

But we weren't just talking about my happiness. We were a team. A family. And families need to thrive together, not just survive in separate emotional corners.

And so, we decided to go back. And then, our plans to return to the mother ship began. Now, of course, the only question was... which one?

Sharon comes from Ireland, and I come from the UK. We needed to decide which mothership we would return to, but we left that decision for later. That this evening was about us. We raised our glasses and recalled our eight years overseas, the laughter, the tears, the fun, the experiences. We'd lived a whole chapter of our lives on this side of the world.

Nobody could take that away from us, not at that moment. Not ever.

Home sickness is a strange thing. In all my years away from the UK, it never hit me the way it hit Sharon. Of course, I missed my family, friends, watching Blackburn Rovers, skiing in the Alps, but I was totally settled here. I felt like I belonged. If any pharmaceutical company invents a homesickness tablet, they will make a fortune, in addition to the ones they already make. Imagine taking a tablet for homesickness, and suddenly you feel okay and that you are already at home. That'd be something.

Anyway, once the decision was made, things moved quickly. Of course, I had to inform ARMS of our plans. I wasn't sure how it would go down, but as luck would have it, they were already looking at opening a European operation, which would fit nicely with our plans to return. That gave us some peace of mind. Next came telling our friends and family, which was probably the hardest part. These were people who had become our everything, our family away from home. Over the years, they'd celebrated with us, supported us through tough times, and watched our little boy grow.

So, we planned a leaving party that doubled up as my 40th birthday celebration. We went all out on a Star Wars-themed fancy dress party. I even built a full-size X-wing fighter (Star Wars fans will know what I mean), and it was parked in the car park of the local golf club with cardboard statues of R2D2 and C3PO standing next to it. The X-wing took a few weeks to build, with the help of some friends. Connor also helped me paint it, and he probably had more white paint on him than the X-wing fighter itself. As a reward for helping his Daddy with the painting, we went into the village to get an ice cream as a treat. One of the neighbours spotted us and asked,

"Connor, why are you covered in white paint?"
With total confidence and a cheeky smile, he replied, "Helping Daddy paint his spaceship".

The neighbour smiled, unconvinced that this was what he was doing. But painting Daddy's spaceship was exactly what we were doing.

The party itself was incredible. Everyone came in costume; there were Stormtroopers, Jedi knights, even a Yoda or two. The music was loud, the laughter was constant, and the dance floor was packed. We sang, we danced, we celebrated not just my birthday, but the amazing chapter we'd lived in this part of the world. It was one of those bittersweet nights, full of joy, but tinged with the sadness of goodbye.
I felt this strange mix of pride and heartache. I didn't want to leave. This wasn't just a place we had lived in; it had become our home. Our life.

But sometimes, you've got to do the right thing for your family.

And so, we said our sad goodbyes: to the beach, the streets we'd walked a thousand times, the familiar faces in the café, the friends who had become our chosen family. We hugged, we cried, we promised to stay in touch.

And then... it was time.

Time to return.

"Homes and machines both run
on small, repeated acts of
attention.
Keep the bolts tight, the
conversations open, and the
courage ready to shut down,
overhaul, and
start again."

Chapter 9

Lubricating Culture, Not Just Machines

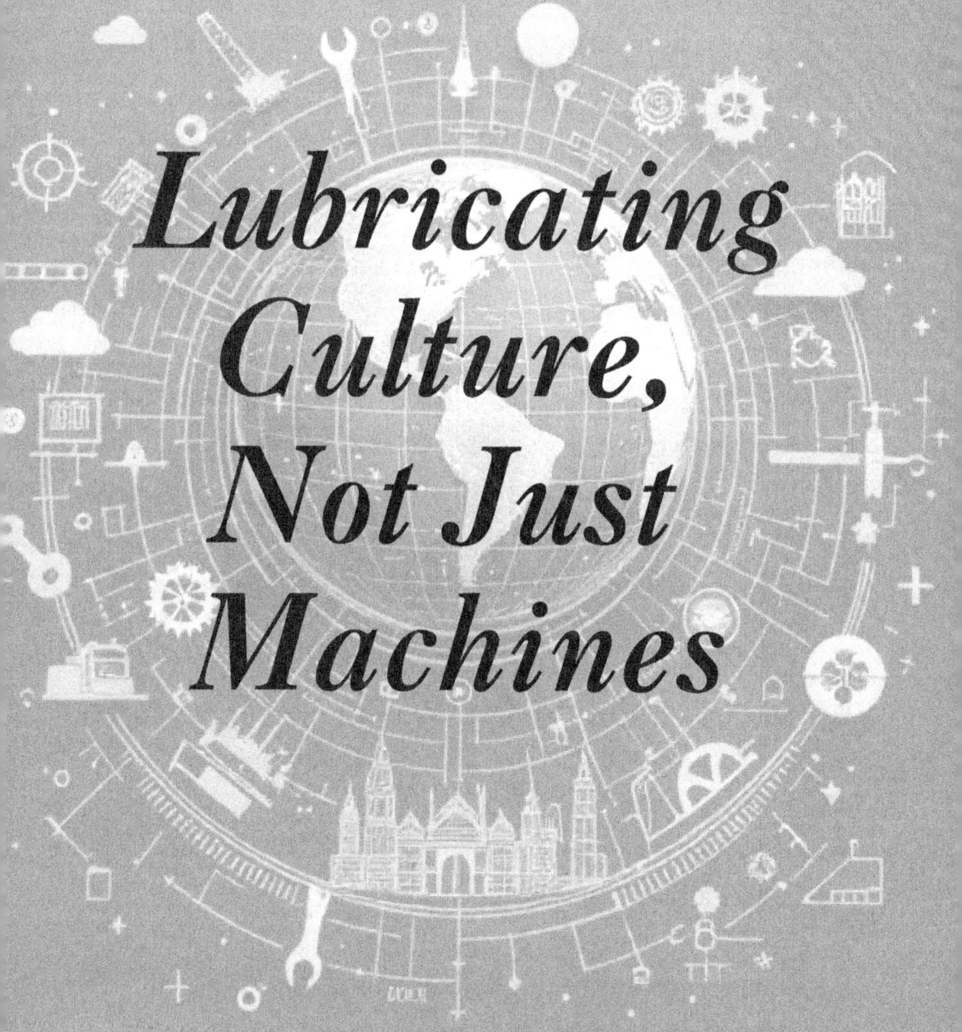

Lubricating Culture, Not Just Machines

"We do not learn from experience... we learn from reflecting on experience,"
John Dewey.

Coming home isn't always as simple as stepping off a plane. It's a collision of past and present, familiar streets with unfamiliar feelings, comforting routines with unsettling questions. After leaving behind the beginning of a beautiful Aussie summer, we arrived back in good old 'Blighty' (The UK) on the 13th December 2008. It felt like we had stepped straight into a wind tunnel, with cold, grey skies and that biting winter chill that makes you wonder why you ever left the sunshine in the first place.

The company directors of ARMS's and my original plan was to get stuck into launching the ARMS Europe operation. It felt exciting, like the next big step. But, as luck or fate would have it, the global economy had suffered an enormous crash; talk about bad timing for our return.

Headlines were full of doom and gloom, and companies were cutting costs left, right, and centre.

Budgets were being slashed, and training was being cancelled. People weren't investing in growth; they were just trying to stay afloat. It became painfully clear that starting a new business for ARMS in Europe was not the right time. The market just wasn't ready, and forcing it would have been like swimming against a tidal wave.

So, after a lot of soul-searching, I made the difficult decision to resign from ARMS. It wasn't easy.

ARMS had been good to me, I had thoroughly enjoyed being a consultant and trainer, visiting different industries, meeting other people and gaining new experiences. It was the best job I had ever had, and most importantly, it allowed me to share my passion for reliability like no other job I had before. Equally, I had also given them my pound of flesh over the years, missing Sharon and Connor's birthdays to run a training course in some remote location in Australia. Looking back, I can admit it: yes, I had prioritised ARMS and my career over my family more than once. That's not something I'm proud of, but it's the truth. And it's important to own that.

Still, I left ARMS with no bitterness; only gratitude. I'd grown so much, professionally and personally. I promised to keep in touch with ARMS, and who knows what the future might bring. My advice is: never burn your bridges.

RENEWED MISSION

Soon after leaving ARMS, I took on a new challenge. I accepted a new role as a Site Reliability Engineer at an ex-ICI factory in Huddersfield called Syngenta. What made it even more interesting was that this site was an ex-ICI site, the same company I had left eight years earlier. It felt like life had come full circle. There I was, back on familiar ground, surrounded by the hum of chemical processes, control rooms, and that unmistakable industrial atmosphere I knew so well. It felt strange.

Stepping into the role, I saw huge potential. I introduced the site to the Apollo method of RCA, along with the Isograph RCM software. Slowly but surely, we started to drive reliability forward. It wasn't about making big, significant changes overnight; it was about making minor, steady improvements that added up over time. In the first year, I had my annual appraisal and came out with flying colours. It was great validation that the work we were doing was making a difference.

Things were picking up momentum, and before long, I was even invited to visit one of their plants in Switzerland to lead an RCM study and train some of the engineering team onsite. I remember leaving the site in Monthey, Switzerland, after a successful week, when one of the engineers asked me when I was flying home.

I told him I was actually heading back to my hotel to pack my bags and would be heading to Geneva later that evening. Then the Engineer told me there are no flights due to the volcano erupting.

I smiled and thought, "What does he mean? There are no volcanoes in Switzerland!"

Still smiling to myself, I returned to the hotel and started packing my bags when my phone rang. It was Sharon. Her voice was urgent.

"Have you seen the news?"
"No," I said.
She said, "All flights have stopped due to the volcanic eruption!"

I paused for a second and told her someone onsite had just said the same thing. That's when I found out about the Eyjafjallajökull volcano (the name I still struggle to pronounce to this day) in Iceland, which had violently erupted and created a dust cloud that drifted towards Europe, causing chaos for travellers around the world. Thinking quickly, I remember saying I would get the train to the Eurostar in Paris and head back from there, but that's what everyone else in Europe had also decided to do. I turned on the news, and it was chaos. Trains and ferry terminals are full of people trying to get home, people fighting for the last tickets to be issued. It was madness. I decided to play it smart. Instead of getting caught up in all the travel chaos, I went to the hotel reception and decided to stay for the weekend. Let the chaos settle down, and I will head back home on Monday, I thought. Except... Monday was exactly the same. Syngenta had its main offices in Basel, and some UK employees were also located there and trying to get home. As agreed by the UK Management team, I would head to Basel and join my colleagues, and we would head back to the UK together. Getting to Basel, though? That was a mission. The trains were packed. Understandable, given the whole "volcano ruins airspace" situation.

I've always enjoyed train travel in Europe, particularly in Switzerland, where trains are notoriously punctual. If your train is 40 seconds late, people look personally offended. The trains don't just run on time; they glide. Quietly. Precisely. The cleanliness of the seat rivals operating theatres, and the coffee onboard? Honestly, better than a lot of cafés I've been to.

And the views!

Through the window, it's all snow-capped peaks, green meadows, and cows that probably have better healthcare plans than most of us. Unless, of course, there is a volcano erupting in Iceland.

When the train pulled into the station, I was feeling optimistic. I had a reserved seat, I was looking forward to admiring the scenery, maybe sipping a glass of wine, and enjoying the peaceful ride through the Alps.

And then...the doors opened.

I had not been able to see inside the carriage because of the dark-tinted windows, and I had no idea what was waiting for me inside... and honestly, I wasn't prepared.

"It was less of a train ride and more of a full-body team-building exercise."

Everyone's standing, shoulders pinned, bags swinging in faces, and someone's elbow is having an identity crisis somewhere near your spleen. I wasn't so much holding the handrail; I was being held upright by the sheer pressure of other travellers. I had reserved a seat, which now feels like a hilarious inside joke. I couldn't even see the seats, let alone get to one. The ticket agent must've laughed when I walked away proudly clutching my reservation. Several hours later, I arrived in Basel. I didn't need to walk off the train; I got peeled out of it.

Eventually, I managed to locate the rest of my Syngenta colleagues, who were also on this unexpected overland trip, very much alive.

Together, we tackled the next leg of our unexpected overland adventure back to the UK. Thanks to the Eurostar in Brussels, we made it back to London safely.

I got back to my office in Huddersfield on Thursday, six days after the volcanic eruption. I felt like a returning war hero. And waiting for me on my desk, courtesy of my colleagues, was a framed picture of Steve Martin and John Candy from the movie Planes, Trains and Automobiles, only my face had been pasted over John Candy's. It said "Welcome back."

LUBRICATION: SMALL DROPS, BIG IMPACT

A plant's lubrication store is a clear indicator of how seriously the site values reliability. That may sound unexpected, but it's true. When I first arrived onsite, it was one of the first areas I wanted to inspect, and, just like in many other facilities, I found lubrication was not being given the attention it deserved.

Lubrication is the lifeblood of a machine. Without proper lubrication, parts wear out more quickly, systems operate less efficiently, and ultimately, machines fail. It's really that simple. Yet, for some reason, it often gets overlooked. Now, I couldn't just walk in and ask to build a new lube store, invest in new equipment and training. That would not work. Instead, we needed to create a business case for the company to invest in this part of the reliability journey.

The first step was to perform a basic lubrication maturity assessment. That means we looked at where we stood compared to what best practice should look like. Once we had that benchmark, it was easier to see the gaps.

With this completed, we assembled a team to conduct a root cause analysis, aiming to understand why our lubrication program was ineffective. We employed the Apollo RCA method, which helped us delve into the root causes of the issues. In the end, we identified 9 root causes for why our lubrication program was ineffective. And more importantly, we developed practical solutions for each one.

Some of the key actions we took included:

- The lubrication project came under the ownership of the Reliability Steering Group. This gave the work visibility and support from leadership.
- Developed a lubrication project plan and budget
- External lubrication support was identified (in this case, it was Martin Williamson from KEW Engineering in the UK – an excellent recommendation)
- Appointed a dedicated lubrication technician
- Identified and built a new lubrication store
- Developed the lube schedule via the FMECA (Failure Modes, Effects, and Criticality Analysis) program
- Implemented the new schedule in SAP

While we initiated the lubrication program, it's essential to recognise that a factory's lubrication practices are often a strong reflection of its overall reliability culture. Lubrication, though frequently overlooked, is fundamental to asset health and performance, and this site was no exception. So, while lubrication was our starting point, we quickly realised the need to address other aspects of reliability to steer the culture in the right direction.

RELIABILITY CULTURE

A reliability culture is all about shared mindset, values, and behaviours within an organisation that prioritise the consistent performance, availability, and integrity of equipment and processes. It's not just about having maintenance schedules or technical tools in place. It's about everyone in the organisation, from operators to executives, understanding their role in keeping things running smoothly and sustainably.

So, what does a Reliability Culture look like?

- People report problems early because they know it's valued, not punished.
- Operators, maintenance, engineering, and management work together, not against each other.
- Preventive and predictive maintenance are part of daily life, not just wish lists.

- Failures are investigated, not blamed, and lessons are actually implemented.
- Data is used for decision-making, not decoration.
- Continuous improvement is a habit, not a slogan.

Reliability isn't just something the maintenance team does; it's a way the whole organisation thinks, just like safety.

A TURNING POINT: GETTING LEADERSHIP ON BOARD

At one point, I started to feel like I was carrying the flag for reliability, but marching alone. I was doing everything I could to drive it forward, despite having little support from site leadership.

I decided to schedule an appointment to meet with the Site Manager. I was welcomed into his office and asked to sit down. "What can I do for you, Gary?"

I knew this was going to be a make-or-break moment in my career; it would either be supported, or I would be told I am no longer required, but I had gone through this scenario before with ICI. I knew the risks and the importance of speaking up.

I looked at the site manager in the eye and asked a simple but powerful question: "Why did you employ me?"

He looked bemused but then replied, "Your experience in reliability is what we need here at the site, to help us become more reliable and therefore more profitable."

He looked at me a bit puzzled and asked, "Why did you ask that question?"

That was my opening. I took a deep breath and laid it out honestly: "I cannot not do it alone. For reliability to be embedded as a culture, it starts at the top, with all leadership on board with what we are trying to achieve. I feel like I was pushing a wheelbarrow uphill, and it is getting heavier and heavier. For this to work, I need leadership support."

He paused for a moment, clearly thinking it over. Then he looked up and asked, "Okay, what can I do to help?"

That's when I handed him a one-page flyer for an upcoming 'Operations Masterclass' delivered in the UK by Ron Moore (Author of Making Common Sense Common Practice). He scanned it quickly, looked at the dates on his calendar and then checked those of his leadership team. After a moment, he agreed that all members of the leadership team would attend this event. Phew, I could breathe again, it went in the direction I hoped it would, and he was very supportive, and for that I was genuinely grateful.

Leadership support on any reliability journey isn't just helpful, it's absolutely essential, even critical when a company is trying to achieve reliability excellence.

Here's why:

1. Sets the Tone from the Top

Without leadership backing, reliability efforts risk becoming just another initiative. Strong leadership sends a clear message:
"This matters. We're committed. This is part of who we are."
It turns reliability from a project to a priority.

2. Aligns Strategy and Resources

A reliability journey requires:

- Training
- Systems (like CMMS)
- Skilled people
- Time for proactive work

Only leadership can unlock these resources and make sure reliability isn't constantly sacrificed for short-term production goals.

3. Drives Cross-Functional Collaboration

Maintenance can't do it alone. You need production, engineering, procurement, and planning, all pulling and moving in the same direction. Leadership breaks down silos and ensures everyone is working toward shared reliability goals, not just their own KPIs.

4. Models the Culture

Leaders who champion reliability, by asking the right questions, rewarding the right behaviours, and being present at toolbox talks, help create a culture where:

- Operators report early signs of trouble
- Planners defend preventive work
- Technicians take pride in root cause analysis

5. Ensures Sustainability

Without strong and consistent leadership and reliability programs often start strong but then fade. Priorities shift, champions leave, and suddenly your Predictive Maintenance (PdM) program is left to gather dust. Support from leadership ensures reliability becomes embedded, not episodic. Sure, leadership isn't about turning the wrenches themselves, but it is about ensuring the right people are doing the right things at the right time for the right reasons. That support makes all the difference.

I had the opportunity to experience this firsthand when I was invited to be part of the leadership team at Ron's masterclass in Cheshire. He was running the class in conjunction with his Reliable Manufacturing partner in the UK, Andrew Fraser. I've recently been doing a series of podcasts with Ron, Andrew and Doug Plunkette on the Mobius Connect Conversation series, which at the time of writing are still available at mobiusconnect.com

During that time, the support from leadership really started to pay off. We started to get more traction with some of the programmes we were introducing. However, after a while, I felt like I was back at ICI, just under a different name. But what about the pace of the corporate world? That hadn't changed. Things happened very slowly, and I was getting frustrated; I wasn't happy. I was missing Australia, I was missing the beach, the barbeques, the sporting banter and even the spiders.

It was tough, and I will not deny it, my marriage was under pressure as a result of this 'homesickness' that I was now suddenly feeling. I was missing home, I was missing the travel, the consulting....my Australian home. I was stuck in a system that moved at a snail's pace, and I was aching for something more.

NEW OPPORTUNITY

Then, out of the blue, a new opportunity landed on my radar. It was a new role called Manufacturing Consultant with the global Automation company Rockwell Automation. They were setting up a new global Manufacturing Excellence consulting team, and I was advised to apply. I had done some work previously in Australia for Rockwell, so I was familiar with the company. Following a few interviews, I was fortunate to be offered the role, and after leaving my role at Syngenta, I started my weekly commute to the Rockwell

Automation UK HQ in Milton Keynes.

The work was varied, and Rockwell had signed an agreement with a company called Meridium, which specialises in Asset Management software. I was looking forward to using this package as I had always been using Isograph, which was deemed a competitor. One of the big perks? I also got to travel with Rockwell. I met the other Manufacturing consultants at a Rockwell conference in Dallas, Texas. That trip stood out to me, not just for the work, but because I got to visit the location of the John F Kennedy shooting and the location of the accused shooter, Lee Harvey Oswald. I guess that killing is still one of the world's great unsolved mysteries and one of the most talked-about conspiracy theories out there.

Back at Rockwell, I was busy promoting reliability both to customers under their Rockwell service contracts and internal staff, including Account Managers. It wasn't easy. Change never is. But we were making progress; slowly, but it was happening.

Rockwell did have an excellent methodology within the services group called the IBE (Installed Base Evaluation). It was a clever method used by Rockwell's services group to assess the risk of spare obsolescence, which could be implemented across a manufacturing facility. And believe me, spares are one of the most overlooked areas in a manufacturing facility's maintenance strategy. When spares go out of date or aren't tracked properly, it can bring everything to a grinding halt. The IBE process helped shed light on that.

SPARE PARTS: THE HIDDEN KEY TO OPERATIONAL SUCCESS

Spare parts management is a critical pillar of reliability and asset management because even the most advanced maintenance plan will fall flat if you don't have the right part in the right place at the right time.

Here's why it matters:

1. Reduces Downtime
When equipment fails, every minute counts. Without the right spare part on hand, even minor failures can escalate into prolonged, expensive shutdowns.

Well-managed spares = faster repairs = higher uptime.

2. Powers Proactive Maintenance
Preventive and predictive maintenance rely on timely access to parts.

Without them, teams are forced to:

- Postpone tasks (risking failure), or
- Cannibalise other equipment (creating new risks).

3. Controls Inventory Costs

Holding too many spares ties up capital and clutters the store with obsolete or unused stock. Holding too few increases emergency purchases and courier costs.

Smart spare parts management:

- Balances availability and cost
- Avoids "just-in-case" hoarding
- Uses data to set optimal reorder levels

4. Enables Better Planning and Scheduling

You can't plan or execute maintenance work properly if you're unsure that the parts will be available on time. A reliable spare parts system builds trust in the schedule, reduces last-minute chaos and supports operational efficiency.

5. Improves Root Cause and Reliability Analysis

Failure patterns often reveal trends in spare parts usage:

- Repeated part failures? It could be due to a bad supplier or an incorrect specification.
- Long lead times? You may need to stock critical spares more strategically.

6. Protects Critical Equipment

High-value assets (like turbines, compressors, or bottling lines) often need specific, long-lead-time parts. If those parts aren't available when needed, entire operations can grind to a halt.

Spare parts management isn't just inventory control; it's risk mitigation, it's about enabling reliability, protecting uptime, and making maintenance work. It's a frontline defence against catastrophic downtime.

BUSINESS TRIPS THE AMERICAN WAY

During my time at Rockwell Automation, I was then invited to attend the Meridium Conference in Roanoke, Virginia. The goal was to get a deeper understanding of how Meridium, a leading asset performance management platform, was being utilised with its customer base. Rockwell was keen to make it the asset management tool of choice in their business.

I still remember the flight to Roanoke; I initially flew to New York with a tight connection to Roanoke. I was delayed by the crazy queues at security and was very close to missing the flight.

I arrived at this small airport in Roanoke and waited for my suitcase to arrive. I stood at the carousel with hope slowly fading as the conveyor belt turned emptier and emptier. Eventually, I had to admit defeat. Whilst I made the flight, my luggage didn't. I reported my missing bag to baggage handling and was told it would be delivered to my hotel later that night. So, I got a taxi and arrived at my hotel with just my laptop bag.

I was utterly wiped out, jet-lagged, suitcase-less, and running on fumes. I crashed out early. Then, at around midnight, my phone rang in the room to inform me that my bag had arrived. I shuffled downstairs like a zombie, collected it (relieved!), and went straight back to bed.

The next morning, I dragged myself out of bed, took a quick shower, and skipped breakfast. Not because I was in a rush, just because my body clock was still in a different timezone and I wasn't hungry. I ordered a taxi to take me to the conference centre, and that's when things got... weird.

I got in the taxi still half asleep, and the driver immediately asked me, "What do you think of 'Osama Bin Laden?".

Not "Good morning" or "Where are you headed?" No, just a straight dive into global terrorism before 8 a.m. Now, I usually enjoy chatting with taxi drivers, but this time, it was too early for a deep and meaningful conversation about international terrorists. I wasn't ready to get into a conversation about the world's most wanted man.

When I arrived at the conference centre, I spotted a coffee bar, so I headed straight there and ordered a coffee to help wake me up. Whilst waiting for the coffee, I spotted a large group gathered around a TV, and to my surprise, I could see a picture of Osama Bin Laden on the screen. I remember thinking,

"What a coincidence, the driver had just mentioned Osama, but I never engaged in conversation, and now his face is on the TV!".

When the server handed me my coffee, she said, "Great news about Osama, huh?"

I walked over to the TV, still piecing it together, and that's when I got the headlines. Osama had been killed in a raid overnight at his house in Islamabad. I remember thinking at that point, I must have been the only person that morning in the USA who was completely unaware of this incident. I hadn't put the TV on in my hotel room. I don't really like American TV; it's full of adverts selling pharmaceutical products. First, they show someone frolicking through a meadow, riding a bike, hugging a golden retriever, and smiling like they just discovered eternal happiness.

Then the voiceover hits: "Side effects may include nausea, dizziness, vomiting, hair loss, loss of hearing, spontaneous combustion, and in rare cases... death."

Wait, WHAT?

You're watching, thinking, "This pill cured her mild eczema, but now she's being airlifted off a mountain because her liver packed up and went to Vegas."

By the end, you don't know whether to call your doctor or your lawyer.

Honestly, nothing says, "trust us" like trying to sell you hope with a smile, then whispering a horror movie in the small print. So, yes, I rarely turn the TV on in hotel rooms in the USA.

After the shock of hearing about Osama, I arrived at the registration desk and obtained my access badge. I was approached quickly by several representatives from Meridium, who were eager to demonstrate the benefits of their asset management software. I had received some training, but I found the software quite cumbersome and slow to produce the final results. I shared this candid feedback with them.

They also knew I was an experienced Isograph user and were curious to see a demonstration of that product. However, I hadn't come to promote; my purpose was to delve deeper into their software and examine some real-world case studies.

Interestingly, when I spoke to other users, their opinion was the same as mine. Many shared the same frustrations. I am sure some of the case studies presented during the conference did get the results being discussed, but to the users in the audience, it all felt a bit like smoke and mirrors.

One evening during the conference, we had the chance to visit the new Meridium headquarters, and wow, what a place! It's a fabulous, converted mill in the centre of town. It was very impressive; they had over 100 software developers in their books!

That was a considerable number and really did blow my mind, considering how cumbersome the software was to use compared to my experience with Isograph. It really made me reflect on how complex software development can be.

As part of the conference experience, they held a 'treasure hunt' competition based on a story from Virginia, which is quite fascinating. The story dates back to 1820, when, apparently, a man named Thomas J. Beale buried some treasure in Bedford County, Virginia. That treasure, made up of gold, silver and jewels, is estimated to be worth over $40,000,000. The clues to the hidden treasure were documented in the 'Beale Papers' published in 1885. These are made up of three encrypted ciphertexts. The first (unsolved) text describes the location, the second (solved) ciphertext accounts for the content of the treasure, and the third (unsolved) lists the names of the treasure's owners and their next of kin.

The story has been made into several TV documentaries. If the story is true, then the treasure is still buried out there somewhere in Bedford County, Virginia.

Anyway, back to our own version of the treasure hunt competition, throughout the conference, attendees like myself were busy attending the presentations and collecting clues. All the answers needed to be handed in on the Friday morning, and at 11 a.m. following conference closing remarks. The winners would be selected. You had to be present to collect your prize. The excitement in the room was surreal.

First, the 3rd prize was drawn, and the lucky winner won a half gold sovereign representing the gold that still remains hidden to this day. Pretty cool!

Then, the second prize was drawn, and it was a full gold sovereign. I was impressed with these prizes and hopeful of being the winner of the first prize.

The winner was announced, "And the winner is...Gary Tyne of Rockwell Automation!".

I couldn't believe it. Wow! I won! Oh, my word!

I must admit that I was shocked, but to be honest, I tend to be lucky in competitions and raffles. I am told I am lucky, and it's true. I've won iPads, mountain bikes, holidays, Apple Watches - in fact, at the time of writing this, I am just on my way back from a Mobius Connect event in Barcelona, and I won a €100 voucher.

The thing is, I do believe in the power of positivity, you know, the little voice saying, "This time, I can feel it, I'm going to win." That mindset doesn't guarantee anything, of course, but it sure makes the experience more fun. And sometimes... just sometimes... raffles or draws aren't about the prize; it's about the possibility.

Anyway, here I am, standing on stage waiting for the big reveal: the mystery first prize. Bonz Hart, the CEO of Meridium and other directors were shaking my hand, smiling, and congratulating me while I waited for the prize to be announced. I was smiling back, trying not to look too eager, but in my head, I was already daydreaming; surely, it's two gold coins?

But then it appeared in front of me.....Wait...what the hell?

A gun?

No, wait, not just any gun, a replica rifle from the American War of Independence. It was complete with a genuine lead bullet fired in the war and a cow horn for storing gunpowder. You could almost hear a distant musket drumroll in the background. They passed it to me as if it were a sacred artefact. And the irony wasn't lost on me; an Englishman, being handed a replica rifle from the war of independence! I could practically hear history groaning.

“Good job, man!" one of the directors, in complete Stars-and-Stripes sincerity, with a deep American accent. There were backslaps, big handshakes, photographs, and so many congratulations. Wow, what a prize that was and all these comments coming straight at me. The American audience's applause was thunderous. They were clapping like it was 1776 all over again. Somewhere deep in my soul, King George was wincing. It would be the same as awarding a Frenchman at a conference in the UK with a ‘Waterloo Gift Basket’.

I remember thinking that only in America could I go to a business conference and end up winning a gun. As someone from England, where even a butter knife can raise eyebrows, the gun laws in the USA appear crazy. Over there, their love of guns is even crazier. Americans love guns the way Brits love queuing and complaining about the weather.

One more memory sticks out, I was at a conference in Florida and having lunch with the Americans at the table. Curiously, I asked those at the table who owned a gun. It turned out everyone at the table owned guns. Out of 10 people, 2 of them had 19 guns each.

Nineteen! I couldn't help myself, I had to ask, "Why do you need 19 guns?"
One of them leaned in, nodded seriously, and said, "Because of them.”

Now, I have an inquisitive nature, and that got my attention.

"Them?" I asked. "Who's them?"
They glanced around, lowered their voice and said, "They're out there."

At that point, I decided I knew enough. I just hope I don't bump into 'them' on my way back to the hotel. As a Brit, I just can't relate to their love of guns; we get nervous holding a potato peeler if it looks a bit sharp.

THE PRIZE THAT NEARLY SENT ME TO JAIL

Travelling back, I thought my wife would kill me when she heard about the gun I had won. She didn't really like me travelling to the USA because people always get shot in their drive-by shootings (well, that's what we see in the news in the UK), and now I have to tell her I've won a gun. To make matters worse, I had a taxi booked in half an hour to take me to the airport from the conference, and I guessed I wouldn't get very far carrying a gun through the airport, unless that's normal here?

So, I turned to Bonz, the guy running the prize draw and said, "Please draw it again, give it to someone here in the USA."
Bonz smiled and said, "No problem. We'll ship it to your address in the UK."

At that point, I actually thought it wouldn't be so bad; it would look nice on my office wall at home. I rang my wife to tell her the good news about my recent bit of good luck at the Conference. There was a long pause. Then she said, "You can't bring that into the house”. I quickly explained it's a replica and can never be fired, it's just an ornament. She didn't seem impressed.

A couple of weeks after I got back from the conference in Virginia, I was settling back into everyday life. Then came a knock at the door. It was the delivery driver, standing there with a large parcel addressed to me. I signed for it and immediately got it out of the box. I tore it open like a kid on Christmas morning. There it was, the replica gun I'd won.

I held it against the office wall, imagining just how impressive it would look mounted up there. All I needed was some brackets and maybe to explain it to anyone who thought I'd joined a militia. But that smug feeling didn't last long. The following day, I had a call from the parcel delivery company.

It was a lady, she said, “Hi, I'm just calling about a parcel we delivered to you yesterday.”

“Yes! I know exactly what it is,” I said, with pride. “It's a prize I won at a U.S. conference, a replica gun. Looks amazing!”

There was a long pause.

"...Hello? Hello?" I said.

There was silence.

She eventually spoke again, sounding a lot less chatty. "I'm really sorry. That parcel should not have made it through our security checks. It wasn't supposed to be delivered. Someone will contact you shortly."

And just like that, she was gone.

A few minutes later, my phone rang again. This time, it was a gentleman from border security or some government department, with a very stern voice. I was explaining how I had won this in a competition, but he didn't even let me finish my story.

"Please stop right there, Mr Tyne," he said. "What you have done is import an illegal weapon for which you need a licence. You have committed a criminal offence which carries a maximum £4000 fine and up to 6 months in prison."

I had heard the saying "my legs turned to jelly" before, but I had never had such an experience until now.

"Oh my god," I whispered.

I could feel the colour draining from my face. All I could think was: this is it. I'm going to jail because I won a raffle. I snapped into panic mode and immediately told him that I had not imported it, I had paid no money, etc I went into defence mode, as I was being blamed for something I had not committed. Whatever I had to say didn't matter. He was all business. And then a new fear hit me.

I could not help thinking, "When Sharon gets home from work, providing I'm still here and I haven't been forced from my house by armed police and helicopters, well, she's not going to be happy!!!"

"Are you there, Mr Tyne.... hello? Hello?"
"Sorry," I replied, trying to catch my breath. "I'm just taking in what you said."

He said he needed me to provide all details of the conference and give the organisers details, and that someone would come and inspect the weapon. I told him it was an ornament, not a weapon. He didn't care. After six weeks of investigation, weeks of stress, paperwork, emails, and phone calls, six long weeks wondering whether I'd end up with a fine, a criminal record, or both.

And finally, after all that, I got the news that I could keep the prize.... and so, it sits gathering dust in my loft.

It never did make it onto the office wall....

Anyway, as I reflect back on my journey now, returning to the UK marked more than just a change in scenery; it was a defining crossroads in my personal and professional journey.

I'd walked away from a role I loved, faced the disorientation of transition, and wrestled with the slow grind of corporate inertia. I experienced setbacks, surprises, and the kind of absurd moments you couldn't script if you tried, yes, including accidentally importing a replica firearm.

But through it all, I rediscovered something essential: resilience.

I had evolved from a passionate consultant to a leader advocating for reliability, not just in systems, but in culture as well.

This chapter, with its turbulence and triumphs, was a necessary bridge between where I had been and where I was heading next. And while the UK may not have felt like "home" in the beginning, it reminded me that sometimes, home isn't a place; it's a point of clarity on your journey, where you pause, reflect, and ready yourself for the next leap forward.

"Grease the bearings,
yes, but also
the conversations.
Reliability begins when we
reduce friction in
how we work,
not just in what we run."

Chapter 10

The Return: Finding My Feet, Losing My Way, & Starting Again

The Return: Finding My Feet, Losing My Way, & Starting Again

"Change your thoughts and you change your world,"
Norman Vincent Peale.

Returning to the UK wasn't just a relocation; it was a reckoning for a couple of years. In this chapter, let's explore together what it really means to come home after years abroad, how it feels to rebuild your professional life while carrying the weight of old ambitions, new risks, and unexpected challenges.

Together, let's explore the highs and lows: the excitement of building something new from the ground up, the risks of travelling through unstable regions, the humour hidden in chaos, and the heartbreak of watching a dream sour. This chapter isn't just about geography; it's about resilience, what happens when purpose collides with politics, when safety becomes personal, and when leadership, for better or worse, changes the course of a career.

So, let's dive in and walk this path together, the return that became so much more than simply being back.

BACK IN THE FLOW BETWEEN TWO WORLDS

Things were going well with Rockwell Automation; it gave me structure, purpose, and a sense of normality. It was a good company to work for; I was on a reasonable salary, and life was going well. I was also starting to come to terms with living back in the UK, and my homesickness for Australia was beginning to fade. But truthfully, it had taken almost three years to feel remotely at peace with being back.

One afternoon, I was visiting a Rockwell customer in the UK. We were discussing Root Cause Analysis, and they asked me if I had any recommendations. Without hesitation, of course, I suggested Apollo RCA, and whilst Rockwell did not have the licence for the delivery of Apollo, I was happy to recommend it based on my personal experience.

Out of curiosity, one of the engineers googled the website, but instead of landing on the Apollo RCA site, he was redirected to a new website with a new name that I did not recognise. I was confused, so I contacted the leader of Apollo in the UK. No answer. Strange. That evening, while I was sitting at home trying to figure out what was going on, the phone rang.

It was Mick Drew, the CEO of ARMS Reliability... and my old boss.

Mick got straight to the point. He was calling to see if I would be interested in starting up ARMS Europe. As it turned out, Apollo was going through a transition, and an opportunity had opened up to continue the Apollo RCA presence in Europe. It caught me off guard. I told Mick I was happy at Rockwell but would think about the opportunity. I enjoyed my time with ARMS in Australia and always maintained that it was the best role I had held. The chance to rejoin and start the European opportunity was probably too good to be true. That evening, I sat down with my family to discuss it.

Not long after that conversation, I made the decision to leave Rockwell and rejoined ARMS in the UK, subsequently setting up their European operation, the role I had initially returned to before the 2008 global economic crash.

It didn't take long to get back into my old familiar role, and my feet had to hit the ground running, with the initial focus to continue to support Apollo RCA customers and build on the Isograph Reliability software relationship. In the time since I had left ARMS in Australia, they had set up operations in the USA. It wasn't long before I was flying out to visit the offices in Austin, Texas, reconnect with the leadership team, and discuss plans for ARMS' European growth. I felt like I was back where I belonged, and who knows, I might even get a visit back to Australia at some stage, my spiritual home.

Meanwhile, ARMS Europe was gaining momentum. The team was growing, and turnover was at a healthy rate. I was getting opportunities to visit other countries within Europe, the Middle East and Africa, meeting new clients, building partnerships, and delivering the kind of work that made me genuinely excited to get out of bed each morning.

ARE YOU JAMES BOND?

One of the most unforgettable experiences during this period was a trip to Tunisia, my first visit to North Africa. I was there to deliver RCA training to a new customer and help set up the program, including trigger points and other key components. It seemed pretty straightforward. The plan was to fly to Tunis and get a driver to collect me from the airport and take me to Sfax, a small town near the Libyan border.

What I hadn't fully considered was that the country had recently been through an uprising and was settling into a new way of operation. I was aware of the vulnerability of being in such a country at this time. Well, it definitely wasn't exactly the safest time to be visiting, but I was told that my travel plans were quite solid and risks had been minimised. So, I thought.

Things started to unravel the moment I landed. The drive to Sfax got changed to a drive to the central train station in Tunis.

Instead of my driver taking me straight to Sfax, I was handed a train ticket and dropped off at the central train station in Tunis. I was also given a card, not a welcome note, but a list of safety rules:

- Don't talk to strangers
- Don't make eye contact
- Don't do this... don't do that...

Let's just say, my confidence took a bit of a hit. I wasn't happy, my plans had changed, and now here I was on a platform in Tunis central station, full of people heading in different directions. It's blisteringly hot. The trains looked like they hadn't seen maintenance since the 70s, and that's being generous. Honestly, I've joked about British Rail before, but in that moment, I would've paid anything for a delayed 7:42 to Manchester.

The platform was crowded, and the smell of body odour lingered in the air. I wanted to Google "Tunisia train safety statistics," but, surprise, I had no Wi-Fi. And then, out of nowhere, a couple started to argue right in front of me. At first, I kept my head down, avoiding eye contact like the card told me to. But suddenly, the young man stopped mid-argument and stared right at me. I am still convinced the argument was set up. I was the only white man on the platform, clearly foreign. I did stand out.

He immediately asked, "Are you from England?"
"...Yes," I replied cautiously.
"Are you James Bond?"
"...No."
"Where are you going?"
"Sfax."
"I'm from Libya," he said.

Then he looked me dead in the eye and said, "You killed my president. Colonel Graffiti."
I blinked. "I'm sorry... who?"
He repeated it: Colonel Graffiti.

Now, I was pretty sure he meant Colonel Gaddafi, but this wasn't the time for corrections.

I just said, "I'm really sorry for your loss," and kept my voice calm.

Before I could process what was happening, the crowd parted like a movie scene. A tall man with jet-black skin, wearing a ¾-length leather jacket in 40°C heat, came striding toward me. Everyone moved aside as he passed.

He was heading right for me. He knew the shorter guy; they spoke. Then he got his phone camera in front of my face, said something I didn't understand, and took my picture. He then turned and walked away.

My immediate thought was: This is it! I am being kidnapped

I will be in the news at 6 this evening, back in the UK: 'British engineer kidnapped in Tunis, negotiations are underway to free him.'

I was very concerned, and my heart was racing.

I remembered I had the emergency card, which had the driver's number in Sfax. My immediate thought was to get a taxi back to the airport and leave asap. I called the guy and he calmly told me to watch the men and if they board the train to inform him. They did board the same train, so I rang my driver again. He said he would have a small red flag and would wave it as the train pulled into Sfax. Then I had to run to him as soon as the train arrived.

I spent the entire train ride on edge, clutching my bag like it was gold. When the train finally pulled in, I spotted the red flag. I ran like my life depended on it; probably because, in my head, it did. The driver grabbed my luggage and bundled me into the car.

Without looking back, he drove at speed to the waiting compound. Armed guards returned along my route to make sure I hadn't been followed.

EGYPT - A TRIP I'LL NEVER FORGET

As part of this client's rollout of Apollo RCA, I was asked to go to Alexandria, Egypt. The plan was to fly into Cairo and then get the train to Alexandria. On this occasion, I had two clients travelling with me (Juan and Keith). We headed out of Cairo and arrived at our hotel in Egypt.

From the start, I was excited. I had always wanted to visit this country and see the pyramids. I had only ever seen them in the movies. I wasn't sure if we'd have time to visit them, but I was quietly hoping we could fit it in on the return journey.

We had a productive week onsite, and the Apollo training was well-received by the team. I even managed to help facilitate a few critical RCAs alongside the newly trained facilitators. Keith, the manager, left a day earlier than I and Juan. Looking back, I still joke that he must have had some inside information about what was coming. Of course, he's always denied this! But I'm still not convinced! Haha! His trip home was uneventful.

The next day, Juan and I took the train from Alexandria to Cairo. A driver was scheduled to meet us at the station and take us straight to the airport. While waiting, Juan said, "We have time to drive past the pyramids? We've come all this way!"

I was hesitant. Egypt had recently had a major uprising, and I heard that it was dangerous for tourists. I suggested we skip the sightseeing and go straight to the airport. But Juan insisted on the detour. The decision was made easier when the driver collected us. He informed us that no flights were leaving that day, and the army had barricaded Cairo airport. Great!

The driver did, however, tell us he knew another way to get us to the airport and that he would circumnavigate the army barricade.

Now that really didn't sound promising... but, in true Juan fashion, he leaned forward and said, "Let's go see the pyramids first."

I must admit I did not realise how close they were to the city of Cairo. As we turned the corner, out of nowhere, there they were, the Great Pyramids of Giza. The view was just amazing!! Seeing the Pyramids of Egypt for the first time is like watching history stand up and stare back at you.

You're expecting something impressive, but nothing quite prepares you for the moment you catch your first glimpse of them rising out of the desert haze. Your brain quietly short-circuits, thinking,

"Hang on... those are real. Like, actually real."

They're massive, not just tall, but heavy with silence, time, and mystery. The scale hits you first, then the age. Over 4,500 years old and still standing prouder than most modern buildings.

You look at the massive stone blocks and think, "How did they move that without cranes, diesel engines, or complaining tradesmen?"

We drove into an armed compound. There were gates, ticket booths, and a military presence. It felt intense. You had to pay to get up close to the pyramids, but honestly, I was happy to just drive by, snap a few photos from the car, and attempt to evade the army checkpoints with our Maverick driver. But no, we had to park up, get out of the car, at which point we were bombarded by self-appointed "tour guides" offering to give us a tour. It was chaotic and a bit uncomfortable.

I went to get the tickets while Juan sorted out the guide. And then, I noticed the silence. There were no tourists. Not one! We almost had the pyramids to ourselves. The place was so quiet. The guide began to walk us around the base of the Great Pyramid. The sun was brutal. It was so hot that I was dripping with sweat, already thinking about how I wouldn't get a shower until I got home. All I wanted in that moment was to be in an air-conditioned airport lounge, with a boarding pass in hand, but here I was being taken in and out of underground rooms that all looked the same.

Then, things took a turn. The guide then took us around a corner, and there, in front of us, was a young boy with three horses, with a huge pile of rubble providing some shade. The guide told us he would take us to see the Great Sphinx. This is a colossal statue of a mythical creature with the body of a lion and the head of a human. I said I wasn't bothered, as I had seen it in the movies. But, of course, Juan was excited.

Then the guide beckoned us towards the horses! I paused. "Wait, I have to ride a horse?" The guide nodded and explained to me that the Giant Sphinx was 12 kilometres into the desert, and travelling by horse was the only way.

I said, "No, I don't ride horses, I only bet on them."

Occasionally (Melbourne Cup, Grand National, etc), I don't trust horses, plus these had flies buzzing around them. But, then again, Juan insisted. He really wanted to go. I couldn't let him go alone, so, reluctantly, I climbed on.

The flies were now buzzing around me. I was wishing I were in the departure lounge. Juan could ride horses; he had them on his parents' farm in South Africa. I had only ever been on the donkeys at Blackpool Beach as a child; now, here I was, riding a horse into the desert to see a statue I really couldn't care about. Juan was laughing; he knew I wasn't happy.

As we set off, my horse steered itself. Which, to be fair, I was impressed with. However, as we emerged around this massive pile of rubble, it was there right in front of us, it had been hidden from view - the Great Sphinx.

For a moment, I was relieved that I wasn't going to be sat on a horse for 12km each way into the desert, but then realised that we had been scammed. In fact, we'd been walking distance from it the whole time. Classic. Anyway, we set off towards the Sphinx. I didn't get the hang of horse riding. I started off feeling like a cowboy, chest out, channelling my inner Clint Eastwood. But ten seconds in, it's less 'Yee Haw' and more "Dear Lord, why is this saddle trying to divide me two?".

Nobody warned me about the bounce. Every trot felt like the horse was conducting a personal vendetta against my family jewels. Juan, ever the cowboy, tried to coach me, but I was just not able to grasp it. The guide then announced that he would take us to see the 'Orchid of the Desert'.

I was like, "What's that?"

Honestly, I just wanted to go back to the driver in the car park. But, Juan was intrigued, and of course was all in. So off we went again, to see this Orchid, me, sweaty and miserable, regretting every life choice that had brought me to this moment.

By now, I am soaking with sweat. My week of reliability and RCA training seemed such a long time ago, and now here I was, heat-struck and saddle-sore. I bet Keith was home by now and sat in his local pub watching rugby, drinking a pint.

Suddenly, a large steel sliding gate was opened after a hushed conversation between our guide and a few security guys. Before I knew it, I was trotting along a 5-lane highway. Yes, an actual road. Cars going in both directions, I had no high-visibility gear, no helmet, cars honking their horns at each other, the fumes and dust choking the air; it was just awful, and my horse just kept clopping forward like it was heading to a medieval joust. I was literally on horseback in rush hour traffic.

"Where the hell are we going?" I shouted at Juan, but he never heard me amongst the noise of the traffic!? He was happy, he loves horses.

Meanwhile, my horse was still steering itself, or it was that well-trained that it knew where this Orchid of the Desert that we were going to see was. The horses suddenly veered right down a side street, then a sharp left. Finally, they stopped in front of a shop. Waiting for us? That same young boy from earlier, ready to collect the horses.

After what felt like hours of bone-rattling chaos, I dismounted my horse like a retired gymnast with hip issues and a newfound respect for cowboys. I walked away bow-legged, clutching my pride (what was left of it), while my horse just stood there looking at me, calm, smug, as if to say, “Amateur.”

We were taken into the shop and offered a can of cold Coca-Cola. Now, I don't even drink Coca-Cola, but I was so dehydrated, I practically inhaled it. It didn't touch the sides. Then, as I looked around, I realised there was nobody else in the shop, not even any tourists. It was air-conditioned, and that was a relief from the heat outside.

The wall was adorned with Egyptian paintings on parchment paper; beautiful, sure, but I was in no mood to buy anything. I was still recovering from the trauma of rush-hour horse riding. Then, a gentleman appeared, cheerful and eager to give a demo of how parchment painting works. Juan got into it and ended up buying one picture, of course.

And then, just as I thought we were done, the man smiled and said, “Now come, you must see... the Orchid of the Desert.”

I froze. Wait, wasn't that supposed to be a place? But, apparently not! We were taken upstairs to a room filled with shelves of glass jars containing liquid. The room smelled very sweet with different aromas swirling in the air. We were told to sit and wait.

I leaned over to Juan and muttered, "I am not happy, and I want to leave. This situation has got out of hand."

Before he could reply, the door creaked open and in walked a tall black man dressed in a pristine white robe. He moved slowly, almost theatrically, and closed the door behind him. And then, in an intense voice, he announces, "Welcome. I am the Orchid of the Desert."

Hang on, I thought I was off to see a rare flower?

But the Orchid was actually a person! What the hell's going on here? He began explaining that all the perfumes were made by rare orchids, and they had been made over many years. He showed us pictures of famous people with him and his bottles of perfume. Then came the samples. When he asked us to try them. I politely refused, but Juan was lathering himself trying to decide which one he preferred. After the smelling session, the Orchid, in his deep voice, said,

"Now you have smelt my perfumes, I need to smell your money."

That was it. I'd had enough. I stood up and walked out, leaving Juan to buy a bottle. I made my way outside, not really knowing where I was going, but I knew it wasn't on a horse.

As I stepped outside the shop, I noticed the horses had gone. Just as I was wondering what to do next, our driver appeared out of nowhere. I got in the back of the car, dazed and dusty. A minute later, Juan jumped in with me, grinning and holding his new purchases like souvenirs from a fever dream. The whole situation was absolutely insane.

The driver set off to the airport, but we did a tour off-road and avoided the army roadblock. I remember sitting there, heart pounding, thinking: "What if they shoot at us?"

I could see the roadblock, and it was obvious what we were doing, sneaking past a military checkpoint in broad daylight. We finally got to the international terminal, only to walk straight into what can only be described as chaos. Crowds everywhere. People shouting. Total confusion. And just like that, I lost Juan in the crowd.

Word started spreading that Egyptian Air was on strike. Apparently, it was their first strike in its history. Seriously? Did Keith know this was going to happen? I tried to push my way to one of the airline desks to ask for further information. Just as I reached the counter, the staff slammed down the shutters. Panic broke out. People at the front jumped onto the desks and started pulling at the shutters. It was starting to get violent, fast. That horse ride in the desert and on the Cairo equivalent of the M25 was serene compared to this.

Still no sign of Juan.

And now I was alone, standing in the middle of an airport riot. I then spotted the Egyptian riot police marching through the entrance further up the airport, carrying truncheons, all wearing perfectly ironed dark blue uniforms. I thought it was time to get out of here. I forced my way out of the crowd and down to the domestic terminal. I got to security and asked if I could access a safe area. They let me through into domestic security. Of course, not before I paid him $100 - I wasn't in the mood for negotiation. I gave him the cash, which he tucked inside his shirt.

Hours passed. I had caught up with Juan again in this area of the airport; he had also made it through safely.

Eventually, someone handed us our boarding passes for the flight to London. I had to carry my bag onto the flight myself. I boarded with no security checks, but was relieved to be out of the airport. Finally, I was heading home. What a day.

Thanks for the experience, Juan!

I've never ridden a horse since, and I have no plans to do so.

The mystery still remains, 'Did Keith know?'

SAFETY FIRST, SO I THOUGHT.

Following these near misses in Tunisia and Egypt, we discussed them at our global HSE meetings. While I can look back and smile at these events and the experiences, they did raise a serious concern about travelling into regions with political instability. I had our corporate travel insurance reviewed. No surprise, we had insufficient cover in these regions.

Apparently, in cases of kidnapping, the most significant costs are associated with paying the negotiators, and not the actual ransom amount. I also spoke with a security specialist regarding travel.

He came up with some useful top tips.

- Carry a false wallet with some expired credit cards and $50 inside it. If held up as a robbery, hand that over, but not your real wallet.
- When staying in a hotel, try to stay on floor 5 or above and below floor 7. Apparently, in countries that have had their hotels attacked by terrorists, they have never made it above floor 5, and the fire services in these countries don't have ladders to reach above floor 7 in case of fire.
- Buy a door wedge for your hotel room. If trouble arises inside the hotel, or for added safety, put a door wedge under your door. If someone tries to enter your room,

> they have no chance with a door wedge. With that in mind and an upcoming trip to Kazakhstan, I purchased a trusty door wedge and packed it in my suitcase. On arrival at my accommodation, I felt safe knowing I had my trusty door wedge at hand. But then, upon arrival at my room, I could not help but laugh. My room door opened outwards into the corridor, making my new door wedge useless.

You see, when you're travelling, safety isn't optional, it's essential. Minimising risks to the lowest level that is reasonably practicable isn't just a box to tick; it's a mindset.

At first, I got the sense that the Australian company had a bit of a "She'll be right, mate" attitude. Very relaxed. Very casual. But things started to shift. Slowly, that laid-back culture gave way to something more structured; we set up a safety committee and began holding regular meetings. It was a much-needed change. Safety wasn't just a topic anymore; it became part of the way we worked. At the same time, things were going well. I was running the European team, which was exciting, but I was very busy and constantly wearing different hats: Engineering Manager, Facilitator, Trainer, HR Manager and even Accounting Manager. It was rewarding, but it was getting out of hand. So, it came as a relief when the ARMS Board of Directors decided to recruit a European Operations Manager to work alongside me and help grow the business.

MY LOWEST POINT

This is probably the hardest part of my personal reliability journey to write about. To be honest, I'd buried it. I had to attend 'mindfulness' sessions to deal with the stress that was created; it took a toll. I could not understand how a company I had worked so hard for could suddenly treat me so differently.

The initial trigger point occurred when an ARMS Overseas Director visited the UK during the recruitment process for the new Operations Manager role. When they told me during a conversation that "I was being paid too much for living in the north of England".

I sat there stunned. Really? That's your takeaway? Not the results? Not the growth? Just my location? I mean, what a ridiculous statement and one that triggered an alarm bell.

Despite my offer to help with the recruitment, I was excluded from the process entirely. I found it strange, even disrespectful. Considering I was running the entire European team and that this person would be working with me to support future growth, surely my input mattered? Apparently not.

Then came the announcement. The new Operations Manager had been selected.

He was from London and would be visiting the team based in the Huddersfield office (North of England). I was also asked to deliver reliability training to this person to get them up to speed with reliability. I met the new manager at the reception and took him to the office to meet the team. What happened next still makes my jaw tighten. He walked into the office, didn't even shake hands with anyone yet, and declared:

"Well, this office will be closing soon. There's nothing in the North; everything happens in the South."

I stood there in disbelief. So did the team. The room went cold.

That comment didn't just offend people; it cut deep. He had managed to insult the entire team, the region, and the culture in one arrogant sentence. How to make friends and influence people? More like how to alienate your whole team in under 10 seconds.

We all thought the same, 'What an a***hole!'

The team in our Huddersfield office was not impressed with this 'southern' attitude, and that moment captured the United Kingdom's North-South Divide at its best.

What is the 'North-South' Divide in the UK?

There's this invisible line somewhere just above Watford, no one knows exactly where, but cross it, and suddenly your pint's half the price and people start talking to you at bus stops.

In the South, you've got your flat whites, artisan sourdough, and houses that cost more than small countries. Everyone's rushing about, no one makes eye contact, and you need a second mortgage to buy a round of drinks.

Then there's the North. Real people. People talk to each other at bus stops. Chips come with gravy, and the weather isn't a complaint; it's a character builder. It's grim up north? Nah - it's honest.

Down South, they say, "Oh, we should do brunch."
Up North, they say, "Let's get a bacon butty and crack on."

So, yeah, there's a divide, but if you ask me, the North's just keeping it real, while the South keeps polishing its avocado. Despite the rocky start, I chose to give the new Operations Manager the benefit of the doubt. It could be nerves or a bad first impression. I kept my head down and stayed focused on the bigger picture, supporting the team and the business.

But it didn't take long to see things weren't going to play out the way I'd been told.

The plan was to work alongside him, not for him. That changed almost immediately. I realised I was now working for him and not alongside him.

I raised my concerns with company directors, who, quite frankly, had mishandled the whole situation.

This new Operations Manager also started to micromanage every minute of my day. He insisted that he received a daily report on the work I had performed. So, I did what he asked. I sent him the report and copied in the directors; not one director asked me what it was for.

I had never once in my career been micromanaged, and if anyone has experienced it, you will know what I am saying here. It sucks the enthusiasm out of you, it kills trust, it crushes initiative, it slows everything down, and ultimately, it drives your best people away. I was one of those people.

With nobody at ARMS whom I could speak with, I felt isolated. My fellow team members could see what was happening. I could feel the stress building. I had never been stressed at work before. This was the best job I had worked in.

I was a key member of the ARMS family, but that was disappearing right in front of me....

After 11 years of commitment, I found myself deeply unhappy and feeling completely unsupported by the ARMS leadership team. Eventually, I made the difficult decision to walk away. There were no farewells, no thank-you, no well wishes - just silence. The door closed, and that was it.

It was heartbreaking. I gave so much, and in the end, I felt discarded. The experience left me shaken, questioning how I'd bounce back.

I was now at my lowest point.

But I now see that 'The Return' was never just about geography; it was about rediscovering who I was through trials, triumphs, and turning points I never saw coming. I travelled across continents, dodged danger, chased pyramids on horseback, and learned the hard way that safety, like trust, should never be taken for granted. I found success, lost certainty, and eventually stood face to face with betrayal from a place I had once called home. But through it all, I grew. I became more resilient, more alert, and more determined than ever to never let someone else define my worth again.

'The Return' wasn't the end of a journey.

It was the start of a transformation.

"In life as in maintenance,
danger sharpens discipline:

protect the system,
respect the limits,
and
never outsource
your safety or your self-
worth."

Chapter 11

Reliability Reimagined

Reliability Reimagined

"In the end, we only regret the chances we didn't take,"
Lewis Carroll.

After everything that happened - the betrayal, the disrespect, the gut-punch of watching my efforts get dismissed - I needed time out. I wasn't just tired; I was drained. The kind of tired that sleep can't fix. So, after having hit the lowest point of my career, I had to switch off. I spend time with my family, walk the dog and recharge my personal batteries. I had lost my enthusiasm, my drive.

I asked myself one honest question: What now?

I didn't know if I had it in me to keep going in reliability or if I even wanted to. But sometimes, when everything breaks down, you get the rare chance to rebuild. This chapter is about that moment.

The pause, the pivot, and the spark that led to something I never expected: the beginning of something entirely my own.

HALF A SECOND TO DECIDE

After a couple of weeks of silence and reflection, I updated my profile on LinkedIn to 'Independent Consultant'. It was more than just a status update. It was me drawing a line under what had happened, stepping away from the past, and opening the door to whatever came next.

To my surprise, that one update lit a spark. I started to get messages and requests for phone calls. These came from within the UK and as far away as Ireland and the USA. I had offers of work, some of which were from previous customers whom I had worked with, and some of which were from new organisations. I was, and still am, very appreciative of those messages of support, conversations, and offers of work. It was humbling. But at this stage, I wasn't sure if I would continue in reliability or take a new path altogether.

Maybe my personal reliability journey was over, and it was time to look at something new. I chose to give myself space. During my time off, I relaxed, attended mindfulness sessions, and read motivational books to help me bounce back. One book I'd recommend is Life in Half a Second by Matthew Michalewicz, which was suggested to me by Jo Wright, author of No More Sh*t Managers (I'd also highly recommend Jo's book for those looking to improve management and leadership in real, lasting ways).

On page 1, Matthew says:

“Planet Earth is four and a half billion years old. The species to which you and I belong, Homo sapiens, did not emerge until approximately 200,000 years ago. The oldest known fossils of modern humans are only 160,000 years old, discovered in Herto, Ethiopia. So, out of the four and a half billion years that this planet has been floating through the nothingness of space, we've been around for some .0044% of that time. Put another way, if our planet were exactly one year old, then modern humans would have only been around for 23 minutes. Measured on the same scale, if our planet were a year old, then your entire life would amount to half a second. In planet time, that’s all you have: half a second.”

"If planet Earth were one year old, your entire life would amount to half a second."

Wow, half a second. I needed to now maximise my half a second.

So, I started looking more seriously at the messages I was receiving. I visited the opportunities in the USA, Ireland and the UK. I was in a very fortunate position, with all my years of experience in asset management and reliability. And then the idea came. Instead of joining another company, why not start something of my own? Why limit my impact to one organisation, when I could help many?

I could do it my way, for the right reasons, on my terms. With encouragement from family and friends, I took the plunge.

After spending three months away from the world of reliability, recharging, reconnecting with my family, and resetting my mindset, I was finally ready to go again. And this time, it was different.

Bring it on!

I dived headfirst into starting my own business. That's when Pro-Reliability Solutions Limited was born.

Starting a business for yourself is much different to starting up a regional office for an international company. Even though I started ARMS Europe with the same amount of enthusiasm and drive as I did when beginning Pro-Reliability Solutions, I knew this time it was different. This one was personal.

This was for me and for my family. They are my 'why'.

My main goal wasn't to build an empire. It was to build a life. My primary incentive was having a work-life balance that allowed me to pay the mortgage each month and enjoy time with family. All whilst continuing with that passion for reliability that I had almost been born with.

It was my destiny.

Soon, things picked up. I was getting busy, trying to juggle a few projects for different customers in the UK and Ireland, while also being invited to present at a few conferences. One of these conferences was in Bangkok, Thailand.

I couldn't believe it. I had to pinch myself. Pro-Reliability Solutions was now going global. Not only was I speaking, but I was also asked to be the chair and moderator for the conference, which was an honour. I also ran a one-day Plant Reliability workshop after the conference. It was packed.

I still remember my opening remarks at the Thailand Conference. I said, "In Reliability, you're only two letters away from being a Liability."

And I explained that reliability is intrinsically linked to safety, quality, the environment, plant performance, and, of course, Profit. And yet we still see so many organisations today that have no clear strategy. No real commitment. No leadership focus. I went on to share something I've learned the hard way:

There is a fine line between Reliability and Liability.

And when that line breaks? The consequences can be costly, dangerous, and reputation-damaging.

Reliability is the promise that your assets, systems, and processes will perform as expected, when needed. However, when that promise is broken, when a piece of equipment fails at a critical moment, or when corners are cut in maintenance, it doesn't just lead to downtime.

It can cross over into Liability.

So, what happens when reliability turns into Liability?

1. Safety Incidents
This is the biggest one. Unreliable systems can lead to injuries, environmental spills, or catastrophic failures or worse. Suddenly, it's not just a machine breakdown, it's a courtroom appearance, an HSE investigation, or a headline in the news.

2. Financial Exposure
Unplanned failures often cost far more than routine maintenance. Then, add in the cost of penalties, insurance claims, legal fees, and production losses, and the actual price of unreliability becomes obvious.

3. Reputational Damage
Customers and stakeholders lose confidence quickly when reliability drops. In industries such as energy, pharmaceuticals, transportation, or food, one failure can shatter years of brand trust.

4. Regulatory Non-Compliance

Failing to maintain assets properly may violate industry standards or regulations, making the organisation liable for fines, shutdowns or legal action.

5. Loss of Talent and Morale

Employees don't want to work for a company where systems fail regularly, and when leadership ignores the warning signs, employees get frustrated. Morale drops. The best people leave. Reliability issues create stress, reduce trust, and damage internal culture.

The truth is:
Reliability is your shield.
Liability is what hits when the shield cracks.

You see, building a culture of reliability isn't just about efficiency. It's a risk management strategy. It's about risk management. Because every time you delay essential maintenance, ignore frontline concerns, or prioritise short-term gain over asset health, you're not just saving time or money, you are moving closer to that liability line.

As I mentioned above, reliability isn't just a checkbox or a process.

It's your shield:

- Against breakdowns.
- Against safety incidents.

- Against reputational ruin.
- Against lawsuits, environmental damage, bad press, and broken trust.

It's the invisible line that holds everything together. And when it's strong, it protects your people, your profits, and your brand.

That's why reliability matters.

I was reminded of this truth again when I spoke at the Thailand conference. It was an incredible experience, sharing ideas, connecting with global leaders, and helping shape the future of reliability.

And since the formation of Pro-Reliability Solutions, I have been invited and have spoken at several global 'reliability' based conferences. Each one has reinforced the same message:

"Reliability isn't just good practice; it's the foundation for sustainable, safe, and successful operations."

Take a look at the table below. Here are just a few of the incredible events I've been proud to be part of:

Conference	Title	Country
Plant Reliability 2018	Reliability Workshop	Thailand
Reliability UK 2018	Key Reasons Why Reliability Strategies Fail and How to Avoid Them	UK
Reliability Ireland 2019	Modelling Condition-Based Maintenance using Predictive Analytics	Ireland
Asset Management Summit 2020	Key Reasons Why Reliability Strategies Fail and How to Avoid Them	Online
Reliability Ireland 2023	Increased Reliability – Effective Problem-Solving using Root Cause Analysis	Ireland
Reliable Plant 2023	RCA v FMECA – Which Comes First?	USA
Maintec 2023	Reliability in Design	UK
Water Ireland 2023		Ireland
Reliable Plant 2024	RCA and Lubrication – What is the Connection?	USA
Exxoconn Dubai 24	Sustainable Reliability Just Got Serious	Dubai
Water and Wastewater Expo 2023	Is your Asset Strategy Optimised for Lowest Cost and Risk?	Ireland
Chem Show UK	Breaking Records Together – Operational and Reliability Excellence	UK
Bakim Istanbul 25	Sustainable Reliability Just Got Serious	Turkey
Mobius Connect 25	Sustainable Development in High Reliability Organisations	Spain
Roll 2 Roll Europe 25	Sustainable Reliability Just Got Serious	Italy
Peak Avenue Conference 25	Reliability Redefined – The Power of Partnership in Machine Performance	Germany

Table 3: Global Reliability Conferences

I've always enjoyed attending conferences and connecting with others to share what 'reliability' can truly achieve when the right mindset and framework are in place. I am also still learning on my own journey, and with every conference, every new connection and conversation, I learn something new. And that's the beauty of this journey. It never really ends.

I have been very fortunate to walk this personal journey of discovery, and I feel that I have a responsibility:

- To give back.
- To help move the industry forward.
- To share the wins, the losses, the close calls, the whole messy, valuable truth.

Because I have lived through the failures, the fixes, the near misses and the unexpected wins. That kind of real-world insight cannot be Googled. By sharing my experiences, I am helping others avoid the same mistakes and accelerate their own learning.

To some degree, that's why I do what I do.
When I speak at conferences...
When I stand on a stage and tell my story...
When I put pen to paper and write this book...

It forces me to reflect. To refine my own thinking. And to honour the lessons that shaped me. More than anything, it gives me a way to give back to a community that's played a huge role in making me who I am today.

In the first year of Pro-Reliability Solutions, I observed something I had suspected for a while. Many organisations were highly fragmented in their approach to Reliability Excellence.

While there were pockets of good practice, most operated in silos. Data was scattered across teams, in spreadsheets, emails, and outdated systems. Reliability culture was inconsistent, and there was little emphasis on structured training or knowledge sharing. As a result, these organisations were often being pulled in multiple directions without a cohesive strategy.

This situation was playing over and over in my mind. Then, suddenly, at 3am one morning, I woke up, I got out of bed and went to my office, I wrote the words 'Reliability Focus' on a piece of paper and went back to bed. It sounds strange, but those words came straight from my subconscious.

You see, when you are awake, your conscious mind is busy with rules, routines and filters. But during sleep, those filters relax. That gives your subconscious mind freedom to explore connections you wouldn't usually make, which often lead to those 'Eureka' moments. And that's what I had just experienced. It's what was missing. A connected digital framework for Reliability. I started to document my thoughts. I was also recommended to trademark ReliabilityFocus™ just in case my thoughts developed further.

Around the same time, Brexit was casting a long shadow, creating uncertainty around trade with Europe. I began considering new opportunities for PRS.

That's when, as if by fate, a message popped up from an old friend and former customer from my oil and gas days - Mark Crosbie. I had trained Mark's team back then, and we'd kept in touch ever since. I always enjoyed his company and still do.

Mark mentioned that if I ever found myself in Ireland, he'd be up for catching up over a pint of Guinness. By then, he had moved back to Ireland with his family and had recently stepped away from his previous role. That one casual chat turned into something much bigger. One conversation led to another, ideas started to flow, and before long, Mark was officially on board with PRS.

That moment marked the beginning of PRS Ireland.

I shared with Mark the story behind our ReliabilityFocus™ concept, a framework designed to help organisations build a culture of reliability.

With Mark's experience and fresh perspective and with some brainstorming, it didn't take long before we had the whole framework in place, the training packages, the standards, policies, and everything we needed to bring this concept to life and the delivery of this framework with impact.

There are, of course, plenty of strong global standards that support asset management.

For instance, ISO 55000 is an international standard that provides an overview of the principles and terminology for asset management, specifically the management of physical assets such as infrastructure, machinery, and equipment. It forms part of the ISO 55000 series developed by the International Organisation for Standardisation (ISO) to promote best practices in asset management across industries. You also have other industry-specific standards, such as IS014224, that are utilised within the petroleum industry.

Other standards for consideration are:

- ISO9000 – for Quality Management
- ISO14000 – for Environmental Management
- ISO31000 – for Risk Management
- ISO50000 – for Energy Management
- ISO14224 – International Standard for the Collection and Exchange of Reliability and Maintenance (RM) Data for Equipment in the petroleum, petrochemical, and natural gas industries

All of these standards are designed to enable industries to apply best practices for improved asset performance, compliance and higher levels of efficiency.

We also have in place the United Nations' Sustainable Development Goals (SDGs), a set of 17 global objectives adopted in 2015 to end poverty, protect the planet, and ensure peace and prosperity for all by 2030. They cover critical areas such as quality education, clean water, good health, gender equality, climate action, decent work, and responsible consumption. The SDGs aim to address the world's most pressing challenges through international cooperation and sustainable solutions that leave no one behind.

Implementing a reliability culture supports the 17 Sustainable Development Goals (SDGs) by promoting efficiency, sustainability, and long-term value creation across industries. A reliability-focused organisation reduces waste, energy consumption, and unplanned downtime, directly contributing to:

- Goal 3 - Good Health and Well-being: by improving safety and reducing accidents
- Goal 7 - Affordable and Clean Energy: by reducing energy waste
- Goal 8 - Decent Work and Economic Growth: through safer, more stable working environments.
- Goal 9 - Industry, Innovation and Infrastructure: by helping communities become more resilient
- Goal 12 - Responsible Consumption and Production: by ensuring safe, well-maintained equipment and systems.

Ultimately, a reliability culture drives sustainable performance, helping organisations make more innovative use of resources, lower their environmental footprint, and contribute to a more equitable and sustainable future.

THE DIGITAL GENERATION IS RESHAPING RELIABILITY

The growth of the internet, social media and mobile technology has affected every aspect of modern working life. Workplace technology is evolving at an unprecedented rate. And it's not slowing down. When it comes to developing a Reliability Culture, there are undoubtedly new challenges to address. However, digital technology is also providing innovative solutions to enable industry and businesses to overcome those challenges.

Millennials were the first generation to grow up with the internet in their pockets. Now, they're a dominant force in the workplace, and they're bringing a digital-first mindset with them. For them, technology isn't optional; it's expected. They're used to apps that simplify life, tools that increase productivity, and systems that connect seamlessly.
And this shift is reshaping company culture. Expectations are changing. The demand for flexible, digital-first environments is expected to increase as younger generations, such as Gen Z, follow closely behind.

So, what does that mean for building a reliability culture in today's world?

TECHNOLOGY TRANSFORMATION

Technology is no longer just a support function; it's a strategic driver. Technology is already having a significant impact on reliability. It means businesses need to embrace digital tools not just to stay current, but to stay competitive. A strong reliability culture today needs to be digitally enabled, from how assets are managed to how knowledge is shared across teams. It means investing in platforms that support collaboration, automation, remote access, and continuous learning, no matter where your people are.

In the past, business leaders have struggled to find ways to increase engagement, improve communication, ensure safe and reliable operations, and continuously deliver high levels of business performance. Digital technology is now available, offering support and solutions that could have only been dreamed of previously. Now it is the turn for reliability and the development of digital management systems and resources to support it.

So, where does developing and embedding a real reliability culture, underpinned by digital technology, fit?

Well, Digital is the bridge. It offers the ability to reach and engage with everyone in a business organisation, closing the communications gap and making the case for change more intimate.

Furthermore, digital offers the opportunity to bring together all of the aspects of a reliability improvement framework, putting businesses and organisations in control of their improvement journey.

At Pro-Reliability Solutions, we help businesses take that leap. Our mission is to support our clients in reaching their potential by embedding reliability as an intrinsic part of their corporate fabric and culture.

Our goal is to help the reliability transition from being something that is "done" to becoming something that is "living" as an inherent part of a business's day-to-day operations.

To deliver and sustain this transformation and achieve reliability success, we are utilising our digital framework, as mentioned above, called ReliabilityFocus™.

Reliability Focus™ is more than a tool; it's a transformation framework. It is an integrated way of working, providing a reliability culture transformation roadmap supported by a variety of integrated modules, programs, tools, and learning experiences that can be customised to suit any particular company's reliability journey needs.

ReliabilityFocus™ is a digital platform that supports embedding Reliability as a culture within an organisation.

Inside the platform, you can:

- Build and manage Reliability Master Plans
- Establish a strong Reliability Mindset across the organisation
- Provide engaging, on-demand learning and development
- Work directly with Reliability Coaches for expert guidance
- Track and monitor your journey to success with real-time dashboards
- Drive compliance and standardisation
- Improve Employee Reliability Engagement

It removes the silo's; it brings teams together to drive forward the best practices required for Reliability Excellence. It brings you culture.

With ReliabilityFocus™, we're not just providing you with a digital platform; we're giving you the blueprint to build a reliability-driven organisation that's built to last.

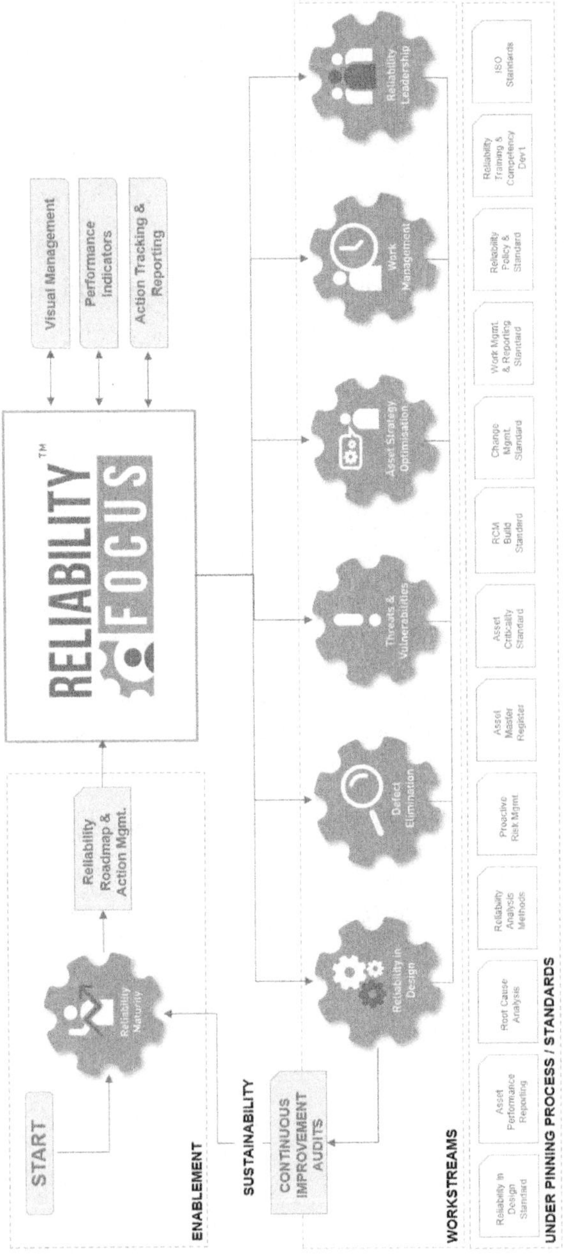

Figure 4: ReliabilityFocus™ Framework

VISUALISING RELIABILITY: THE POWER OF THE VIADUCT

At some point, several customers asked me a really interesting question:

"How can we represent reliability in a way that's simple and easy to understand?"

We often talk about the official definition of 'Reliability' and we all know the textbook definitions, but how could we represent it with a single picture?

It got me thinking.

Something I have always been fascinated by something I seek out whenever I travel, is bridges and viaducts. To me, they are not just structures, they are a powerful blend of engineering, beauty, history and human ambition. They conquer rivers, valleys, gorges, all places we were never meant to cross easily. And yet, somehow, we do.

Bridges and viaducts transform natural obstacles into connections, allowing humans to continue their journey. For me, they remind us of what's possible when creativity, necessity and engineering collide. They make the impossible – crossable.

And in many ways, that's exactly what a reliability journey is all about.

The viaduct is a symbol of the reliability journey.

Just as a viaduct bridges vast gaps between two distant points, over valleys, rivers, or rough terrain, a reliability journey bridges the gap between where an organisation is today and where it truly wants to be. Whether you're currently stuck in a reactive, siloed, or firefighting mode, or just struggling with inconsistency, the goal is to reach a state of proactive, efficient, and high-performing reliability.

You don't cross that valley in a single leap.

You build it. One step, one pillar, one foundation at a time. That's precisely what the ReliabilityViaduct™ represents. It’s a visual, structured way to understand how reliability comes to life inside an organisation. It illustrates the key pillars of a reliability journey, represented here as a viaduct. Without strong pillars, the viaduct will collapse and along with it, so will the reliability journey.

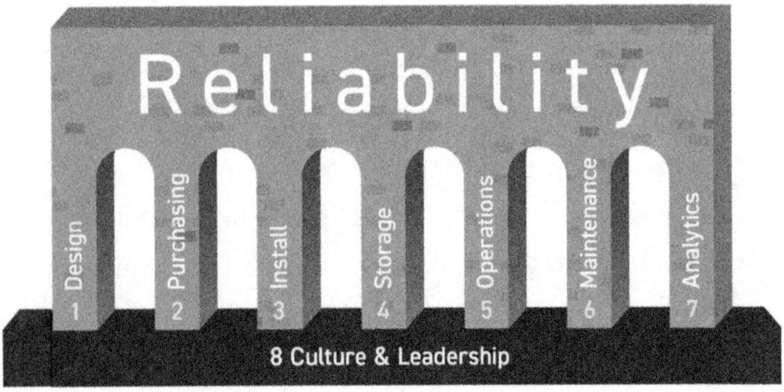

Figure 5: The ReliabilityViaduct™

When it comes to explaining what reliability really means and what it takes to achieve it, we believe in keeping things simple, visual, and relatable. We use the simple ReliabilityViaduct™, with its pillars of reliability maintaining and giving the viaduct its strength and longevity. But no viaduct stands on its own. It needs strong, dependable pillars. And so does your reliability strategy.

Let's take a closer look at the seven key pillars of the ReliabilityViaduct™, and the essential foundation that holds it all together.

Pillar 1 - Design: As mentioned above, the importance of considering reliability in the design phase cannot be overemphasised. It's the beginning of the assets' journey towards production, and it's where the most critical reliability decisions are made. If we ignore reliability at this stage, then you're locking in future problems. You can't bolt on reliability later. You can't out-maintain poor design, because more maintenance further down the track will not necessarily provide more reliability.

Pillar 2 - Purchase: Buying cheaper, lower-quality components might seem like a smart cost-saving move in the short term, but it's a trap. If you purchase inferior parts and cheaper components, these will cause problems that eventually will lead to downtime and unplanned events.

OEM parts or other high-quality items would always be recommended. I remember using the following quote by John Ruskin in a presentation at ICI many years ago. It's still applicable today:

"It's unwise to pay too much, but it's worse to pay too little. When you pay too much, you lose a little money; that's all. When you pay too little, you sometimes lose everything, because the thing you bought was incapable of doing the thing it was bought to do. The common law of business balance prohibits paying a little and getting a lot - it can't be done. If you deal with the lowest bidder, it is well to add something for the risk you run, and if you do that, you will have enough to pay for something better"

You see, reliability requires investing in quality. Every purchasing decision is a vote for or against your future performance.

Pillar 3 - Installation: If you don't install it right, it won't run right. If an asset is improperly installed, it may operate under stress, misalignment, or imbalance from day one. This leads to premature wear, higher energy consumption, and early failure, even if the asset itself is well-designed. Precision installation is the foundation of reliability in early life. If you don't start with precision, everything else, monitoring, maintenance, and management, is just damage control.

Pillar 4 - Storage: Treat your spare parts like live assets. Storing spare parts in the right conditions is crucial because poor storage can turn valuable, ready-to-use components into expensive, unreliable liabilities. Rubber, plastics, lubricants, electronics, and seals degrade quickly if exposed to heat, humidity, UV light, or dust. Bearings, for example, can rust or suffer false brinelling from improper storage, even without being used. Look after your spares and they will look after you.

Pillar 5 - Operate: Every asset is designed to perform within a specific range, known as its "design envelope." The "design envelope" refers to the specific operating conditions, like temperature, pressure, load, speed, and environmental factors, within which the equipment is engineered to function reliably. Operating equipment outside its design envelope introduces serious risks to reliability, safety, and performance.

Pillar 6 - Maintain: Smart maintenance is about timing, not just action. Maintaining equipment at the right frequency and with a clear understanding of failure modes and maintenance tasks is crucial because it directly influences asset reliability, safety, cost-efficiency, and operational continuity. Too frequent maintenance wastes resources and may introduce new failure risks. Too infrequent maintenance risks unexpected failures, higher downtime, and costly repairs.

This section also includes maintenance planning. Without planning, reliability becomes guesswork. Maintenance planning and scheduling are essential for achieving reliable, efficient and cost-effective operations. Without them, maintenance becomes reactive, chaotic and unnecessarily expensive.

Pillar 7 - Analytics: Analysing reliability data is essential to ensure we not only capture information but also translate it into meaningful action. Data on its own holds little value unless it is used to drive decisions, improvements, and communication across the organisation. Without action, valuable time and opportunities are lost. That's why it is critical to establish a clear strategy for reliability, one that provides direction, supports decision-making, and reinforces the understanding that reliability is not a one-off task, but a continuous journey of improvement.

FOUNDATIONS: 8 - CULTURE AND LEADERSHIP

Culture is the ground upon which everything stands.

You can have the best systems, tools, and strategies, but if the culture isn't right, none of it sticks. Having the right organisational culture within maintenance and reliability is essential because culture drives behaviour, and behaviour determines outcomes.

A positive reliability culture:

- Fosters a proactive mindset.
- Encourages people to prevent, not just fix.
- Promotes ownership and accountability.
- Shifts thinking from "What failed?" to "Why did it fail and how can we stop it happening again?"

At Pro-Reliability Solutions, we know that true reliability isn't just built on technical skills; it's built on a mindset. That's why culture and leadership is the foundation of the ReliabilityViaduct™. Get the culture and leadership right, and the pillars will hold strong for the long haul.

MY 40TH YEAR – A MILESTONE, A MOMENT, A MISSION

And just like that, here we are: 2025.

This year marks my 40th year in the world of maintenance and reliability. Four decades of learning, doing, failing, fixing, building, leading, and, above all, discovering.

I am about to head over to New Zealand and Australia with my family, to visit old friends and squeeze in a few business meetings along the way. I find myself looking back with gratitude... and forward with fresh determination. It was during my long-haul flight that I decided to set some new goals and challenges for this special year.

The first is to climb the three highest mountains in the UK. So far this year, I've climbed Scafell Pike, the UK's highest. I have Snowdon (Wales) and Ben Nevis (Scotland) in my calendar for later this year.

The second challenge: writing a book to celebrate my 40th year. I set out not wanting to write another book on RCM, World-Class Maintenance, Asset Management, or Root Cause Analysis, as there are already plenty of excellent books covering those topics. Equally, I did not want it to be a technical book; I wanted something more personal, more human. I wanted to embrace it with a collection of stories, lessons and reflections from a lifetime spent in this incredible profession.

You see, this book is not just about machines, it's about the people behind them. It's about what works and what doesn't, about learning from mistakes, celebrating the wins, seeing the highs and lows, the tears and laughing at the moments that felt like anything but funny at the time. It's about the real journey behind the charts, KPIs, and improvement programs.

Most importantly, I wanted to create something that makes you feel like you've been on a personal journey of discovery in the world of Maintenance and Reliability with me, whether you're just starting out or have decades of experience under your belt.

If it's made you smile, made you think, or reminded you of your own stories, then it's already done what I hoped it would.

And to close out this chapter and open the next, I wanted to share something special. So along with all the stories, tips and advice I have given in this book, in the next chapter, you'll find 40 lessons from my 40 years in Maintenance and Reliability.

Some are practical.
Some are philosophical.
Some are pulled straight from the stories you've already read.

But all of them are real. Tested. Lived. Earned.

So, whether you read them one by one or dive in all at once, I hope they give you something valuable, something to carry into your own journey, wherever it leads.

Because after 40 years, if there's one thing I know for sure, it's this:

Reliability is not just what you do, it's how you think, how you lead, and how you live.

Let's get into the lessons...

"When my career broke down,
I learned the greatest
truth of reliability:

Every failure is also a chance
to rebuild stronger,
with better design,
deeper purpose,
&
more heart."

Chapter 12

40 Lessons in 40 Years

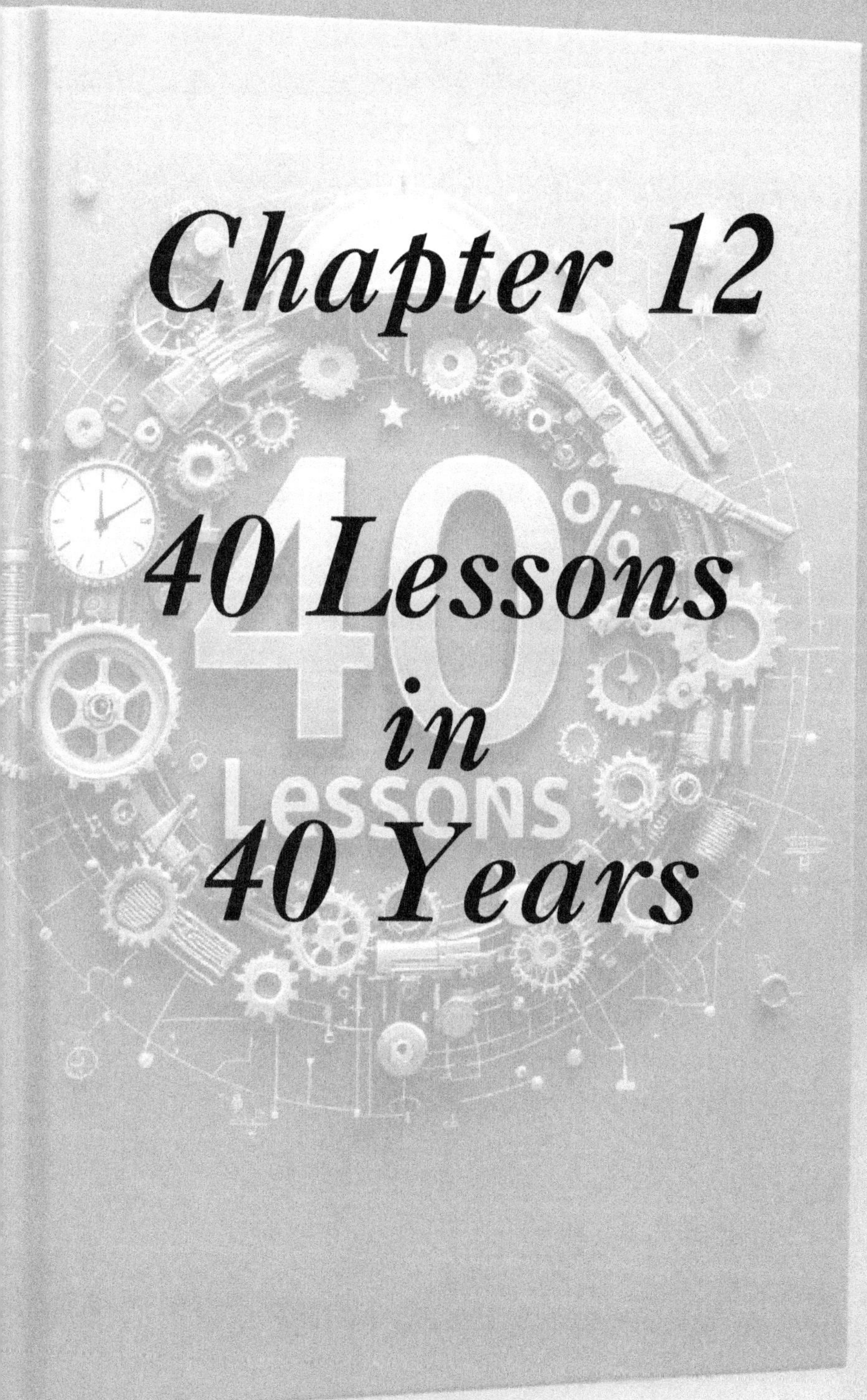

40 Lessons in 40 Years

"The only real mistake is the one from which
we learn nothing,"
Henry Ford.

Forty years. That's how long I've walked this road, through factories, boardrooms, breakdowns, and breakthroughs. Thank you for sticking with me and following my journey through the world of Reliability and Maintenance. Truly. Thank you. You've seen the highs, the hard lessons, and the honest reflections. I don't take your attention or your time for granted.

What I'm about to share isn't theory; it's experience. These lessons were shaped on the ground, through real challenges, real people, and real consequences. While they're personal to me, I know they'll resonate with anyone who's spent time in the trenches of operations, maintenance, and leadership.

Reaching the 40-year mark forces you to pause.

To look back and ask: What truly mattered?

40 Lessons in 40 Years

Over the past four decades, I've had the privilege and challenge of witnessing the evolution of reliability practices across various industries, teams, and leadership styles. I've made my share of mistakes, learned the hard way, and gathered insights that now shape how I lead, think, and support others on their own journeys.

Capturing those lessons wasn't simple. What started as a chaotic brain dump of notes scribbled down, memories triggered by old photos, and frustrations eventually began to reveal patterns. These weren't just scattered thoughts. These weren't just random insights; they fell into themes that echoed across departments and decades, and they fell into themes that repeated across the years.

That's when I realised, these lessons needed structure. Not just to make sense of them for myself, but to make them easier for you to use and apply. So, I grouped them into eight categories, each with five key lessons. They're not perfect. But they are real. And they come from the places where theory meets reality, on plant floors, during late-night failures, in cross-functional meetings, and in moments when people decided to do the right thing, even when it was hard.

So here they are: 40 lessons in 40 years.

Use them. Share them. Question them. Most importantly, let them start conversations in your own journey, whether you're just getting started or already leading from the front. Take what resonates, challenge what doesn't, and make them your own.

PART 1: ORGANISATIONAL CULTURE & LEADERSHIP

1. Reliability Starts with Culture, Not Tools

True reliability is rooted in mindset, not machinery. No tool, technology, or strategy can fix a poor culture. A team that values reliability will outperform any high-tech system operating in a toxic environment. Invest in people first. Build a culture where reliability is a shared value, not a checkbox. Only then will tools become force multipliers, rather than crutches.

2. Leadership Commitment Drives Sustainable Change

Without leadership buy-in, reliability initiatives are short-lived. When leaders visibly champion reliability not as an isolated engineering objective, but as a core business value, it signals to every level of the organisation that reliability matters. Just like safety, it becomes a non-negotiable standard rather than a nice-to-have. Leadership commitment fuels alignment, secures resources, and embeds accountability.

It transforms reliability from a technical afterthought into a strategic pillar that supports customer trust, operational excellence, and long-term success.

3. Free Environments Encourage Truth and Improvement

Blame is the enemy of progress. Fear of punishment leads to cover-ups and missed opportunities. Cultivating a culture where failures are seen as learning opportunities empowers teams to surface issues early and often. Ultimately, a culture that prioritises learning over punishment builds not only more resilient systems but stronger, more engaged people behind them.

4. Micromanagement Kills Ownership and Accountability

Micromanagement is the silent killer of accountability. Leaders who micromanage not only create dependency and kill motivation, but they also erode confidence, creativity, and commitment. Empowered teams take ownership of reliability outcomes because they're trusted to make decisions and contribute ideas. They don't just follow instructions; they invest in results.

Great leaders don't manage tasks; they cultivate leaders at every level by giving people the space to own their work and grow from it.

5. Celebrate Small Wins to Build Reliability Momentum

Significant transformations are built on the back of small, consistent victories. Celebrations reinforce good habits, energise teams, and make people feel part of something bigger, consequently reinforcing the behaviours that drive progress.

PART 2: RELIABILITY IN DESIGN

6. Design for Maintainability and Access

Reliability starts at the design table. When assets are built without considering the people who maintain them, even the best systems are destined to fail. Poor access, hard-to-reach components, or non-standard parts turn minor repairs into major jobs. When design prioritises the maintainer's experience, minor issues stay minor, response times shrink, and reliability becomes a natural outcome, not a constant struggle.

7. Standardisation Beats Complexity Every Time

In the pursuit of reliability, simplicity wins. Standard parts, tools, and systems reduce training time, spare parts inventory, and error rates.

They shorten training curves, minimise errors, and streamline decision-making under pressure. Complexity, on the other hand, is a hidden cost that compounds over time. Standardisation isn't about rigidity; it's about clarity, repeatability, and control. The more uniform your systems, the more resilient and agile your organisation becomes when it matters most.

8. Involve Operations and Maintenance Early in the Design Process

Frontline insight is a strategic advantage, yet too often, it's brought in too late. When maintenance and operations teams are excluded from the design phase, critical practicalities are often overlooked, including access issues, safety risks, excessive wear points, and hard-to-service components.

Getting their input early avoids costly rework and operational pain later.

9. Overdesign Without Justification is a Hidden Liability

More isn't always better. Overengineering drives up costs, increases maintenance complexity, and can introduce new failure modes. True engineering excellence lies not in how much you can add, but in how much you can simplify without sacrificing function.

10. Lifetime Cost Matters More Than Initial Cost

The cheapest option up front often becomes the most expensive in the long run. The initial purchase price is just a fraction of the total asset cost. Factoring in energy use, spare parts, labour, and downtime is essential for long-term value. Focusing solely on capital expenditure blinds organisations to the actual cost of ownership. Smart, reliability-focused decision-making demands a long-term lens. That means evaluating total lifecycle value, not just sticker price.

PART 3: PURCHASING & PROCUREMENT

11. Don't Outsource Your Reliability to the Lowest Bidder

Reliability cannot be bought cheaply, and it certainly can't be outsourced to the lowest bidder without consequence. When procurement decisions and vendor choices are driven solely by cost, you invite poor performance, subpar materials, inconsistent quality, and vendors who disappear when problems arise. Choosing vendors based exclusively on cost can lead to poor performance. Instead, partner with suppliers who understand and support your reliability goals.

Choose partners, not just providers.

12. Technical Specifications Must Match Operational Reality

Procurement teams need to ensure that technical specifications align with the real-world environment the equipment will face. Buying equipment that doesn't match conditions leads to premature failure.

13. Ask for Reliability Data When Buying New Equipment

When buying new equipment, don't just take the vendor's word for it. Demand data on performance, failure history, and maintenance from vendors. If they can't provide it, question why. Reliable equipment comes with a track record. Don't invest your plant's future in guesswork.

14. Involve End Users in Procurement Decisions

No one knows the equipment better than the people who work with it every day. Operators and maintenance teams understand what works and what doesn't. Their insights can prevent poor purchasing decisions that look good on paper but ultimately fail in practice. So, always involve end users; they're your best insurance against buying the wrong asset.

15. Total Cost of Ownership Must Drive Procurement Strategy

Short-term savings can lead to long-term pain.

Cheap equipment can come with hidden costs: more breakdowns, more maintenance, more downtime. Smart procurement considers the total cost of ownership, encompassing the entire lifecycle, from installation to end of life. This holistic view of asset cost, including maintenance and downtime, protects operational and financial performance.

PART 4: INSTALLATION & COMMISSIONING

16. Install It Right, or Pay for It Later

Poor installation is a leading cause of early failure. Even the best equipment will fail early if it's installed poorly. Bad alignment, loose connections, and missing steps; these small mistakes become significant breakdowns. Follow standards, verify quality, and never cut corners. Every shortcut taken during installation becomes a future maintenance problem.

17. Factory Acceptance Tests (FATs) Are Not Optional

FATs catch issues before equipment leaves the vendor's facility. Skipping them is like buying a car without taking it for a test drive. If something's going to go wrong, you want it to happen before it's on your floor, not after.

18. Commissioning Must Be a Cross-Functional Responsibility

Commissioning must involve engineering, maintenance, and operations together. Each team brings a different lens: design, upkeep, and day-to-day use. When these groups work in silos, important details often get overlooked. When they work together, they catch problems early and set the equipment up for long-term success.

19. Build Reliability into the Handover Process

Handovers shouldn't just be paperwork. It's your chance to set the tone for asset reliability. This means delivering comprehensive documentation, training, asset data, spare parts lists, and a walkthrough of critical functions. When handovers are thorough, teams are prepared. When they're rushed, mistakes multiply.

20. Training During Commissioning Avoids Decades of Error

Poor habits formed early are hard to undo. Training operators and maintainers during commissioning builds good practices from day one. Get it right early, and you won't spend the next 20 years fixing preventable mistakes.

PART 5: STORAGE & SPARE PARTS MANAGEMENT

21. Poor Storage Equals Planned Failure

Spare parts left in the wrong conditions, exposed to moisture, heat, dust, or time, are already halfway to failure before they're even used. Rusted bearings, hardened seals, expired electronics... they'll all let you down when you need them most. Proper storage is low-cost insurance for high-cost equipment. Treat your spares like the assets they are.

22. Classify Critical Spares, Don't Stock Everything

Not every part deserves a spot on the shelf. By classifying spares based on criticality, you can focus on what truly matters, reduce inventory costs, and free up valuable capital.

23. Digital Spare Parts Records Must Be Accurate

On a breakdown, there's no time for guesswork. Mismatched records and phantom stock lead to chaos during breakdowns. An accurate CMMS is a lifesaver when it is accurate and up to date. That means regular audits, good data entry, and disciplined processes.

24. Parts Obsolescence is a Time Bomb

One day, a critical component fails, and you discover it's no longer manufactured. That's not bad luck. That's a preventable crisis. Outdated components can bring modern equipment to a halt. Monitoring obsolescence and planning replacements avoids emergency retrofits.

25. Stockouts Happen When You Trust Tribal Knowledge
Relying on memory or experience instead of a system can lead to disaster. Systems, not heroes, should manage spares.

PART 6: PRODUCTION AND OPERATIONS

26. Operators Are the Eyes and Ears of Reliability

Operators detect subtle changes before sensors do. Their experience and observations are vital to early problem detection. Operators are your frontline defence against failure. Treat their observations as early warnings, not afterthoughts. If they speak up, listen.

27. High Frequency, Short Duration Faults Are Silent Killers

Minor stoppages often get ignored, but they often indicate deeper issues: problems,misalignment, wear, and control problems.

If left unchecked, over time, they erode performance and lead to bigger failures. Don't ignore the small stuff; it's often the start of something big.

28. Bad Habits Become the New Normal Without Checks

When operators work around issues, those workarounds become routine. That's human. But when those shortcuts become routine, you've created invisible risk. Workarounds must be surfaced, reviewed, and either formalised or eliminated.

29. Production Pressure Often Undermines Reliability

When the focus is only on output, maintenance and inspections get skipped. This short-term gain leads to long-term pain. Maintenance and Production aren't enemies; they're partners. Sustained output depends on disciplined maintenance, even under pressure.

30. Operator Training Must Include Failure Modes

Operators should know what can go wrong and why. Understanding equipment failure modes enables them to become active contributors to reliability, and also active participants in prevention. This empowers operators to identify early signs, take more informed action, and protect the asset. Train operators in failure mode identification.

PART 7: MAINTENANCE & ASSET CARE

31. Planning and Scheduling Beat Reactive Chaos

Unplanned maintenance is always more stressful, more expensive, and more dangerous. Planned work is safer, cheaper, and faster. Scheduling maintenance ensures resources are ready and downtime is minimised.

32. Maintenance Tasks Must Match Failure Modes

Not all maintenance is useful. If the task doesn't address a real failure mode, it's wasted effort. Use RCM principles to match the right tasks to the right risks, on the right equipment, for the right reasons.

33. Predictive Maintenance is a Tool, not a Silver Bullet

Condition monitoring is powerful, but it's not magic. It's just one tool in the toolbox, and it should support, not replace, basic good maintenance.

34. Clean Machines Last Longer - 5S is Not Just for Show

A clean environment exposes leaks, wear, and misalignment early. Cleanliness is the frontline of defect elimination.

35. Lubrication is the Lifeblood of your Machines

It reduces friction between moving parts, preventing wear and overheating. Without proper lubrication, components grind, seize, and fail prematurely, just like a heart without blood, a machine without lubrication doesn't last long. So, ensure good lubrication practices are in place.

PART 8: STRATEGY, ANALYTICS & CONTINUOUS IMPROVEMENT

36. Data Without Action is Just a Missed Opportunity

Collecting data is easy. Acting on it consistently is what creates value. Dashboards don't improve reliability. Decisions do. If you're not using your data to drive action, it's just decoration.

37. Work Orders Are Gold Mines for Reliability Data

Each work order holds clues to improve performance. It contains insights about failure patterns, equipment condition, and human performance.

Dig into them; they're gold mines for improving your processes and avoiding repeat problems.

38. RCA is Learning, Not Blaming

RCA isn't about pointing fingers. It's about understanding why something went wrong so it doesn't happen again. When done right, RCA strengthens your systems, your people, and your culture. Train people in a structured RCA process.

39. Benchmark, But Don't Copy-Paste Solutions

Other companies can inspire you, but every organisation is unique. Adapt ideas, don't blindly adopt them. Benchmark your organisation, build a reliability roadmap and implement the journey.

40. Reliability is a Journey, not a Project

There's no finish line in this work. Reliability requires ongoing commitment, feedback, and evolution. It's a long game, but one that pays off in performance, pride, and peace of mind.

And so, there they are, 40 lessons distilled from 40 years; a lifetime in reliability, leadership, and learning. Now, this chapter is not the end of anything; it's the start of deeper reflection. Each lesson carries scars and successes. Some learned the hard way, while others learned through mentorship, collaboration, and listening to those closest to the work. It has been a long but rewarding 40 years on this journey filled with ups and downs, challenges and triumphs, laughter and a few tears; it all comes down to these 40 lessons.

I offer them to you not as a rulebook, but as reflections forged through experience. Use them in your organisation, share them with your teams, discuss them in meetings, print them out, pin them up, and make them part of your conversations. Because every one of them came from a real problem, a real team, and a real moment where reliability either failed or flourished.

These are my lessons, now they're yours.

Some may echo your own journey, while others may challenge your thinking; however, all are shared with the hope that they'll spark insight, growth, and better outcomes for you, your people, and your organisation.

"Wisdom isn't what you know; it's what you apply, share, and pass on. Reliability is built the same way: one lesson, one choice, one conversation at a time."

Chapter 13

The Next Chapter is Yours

The Next Chapter is Yours

"The journey's end is not where we stop, but where we hand the torch to those who follow."
Anonymous

I did not want to call the final chapter 'The End' because it's not. Not for me, and hopefully, not for you either, because this personal journey of discovery continues.

This journey, my personal path through Maintenance and Reliability, has lasted over four decades. But in many ways, it feels like it's just getting started again. The tools may be changing, the pace may be quickening, but the mission remains the same: to keep things running, smarter, safer, and more sustainably than ever before.

THE WORLD IS CHANGING, FAST

We're living in an era of constant innovation.

The world of technology, machine learning, Artificial Intelligence (AI), digital twins, and smart sensors is all out there making a difference to how we design and maintain machines.

With AI-powered predictive analytics, factories can move beyond traditional time-based maintenance to data-driven strategies that identify issues before they become failures. AI can spot patterns across vast datasets, optimise spare parts inventory, suggest the most effective tasks, and even automate routine diagnostics, all in real time.

The result?

Less unplanned downtime, better resource utilisation, and smarter decision-making, all while freeing up human teams to focus on higher-value work. It's a massive leap forward. However, here's the thing I've learned:

"If your basics are broken, no technology in the world will save you."

Getting the basics right is critical before adopting advanced technologies like AI. Without foundational maintenance practices such as good lubrication, accurate asset data, effective planning, and disciplined work execution, AI will simply analyse bad inputs and deliver unreliable outputs.

Think of AI as a performance amplifier; it only multiplies what you already have.

Which means, it only works well if the underlying maintenance system is already sound. Before chasing shiny tools, ensure your foundations are solid. That's not old-fashioned thinking. That's sustainable thinking.

STORIES OVER THEORY

There's something I've come to believe deeply over the years:

Real stories beat theory. Every time.

Yes, the industry of Maintenance and Reliability Conferences is full of models, frameworks and acronyms, but it's the stories that people remember.
People don't remember models or acronyms; they remember stories.

Stories are what stick:

- How we boosted uptime after a crushing failure
- How we rebuilt trust between engineering and operations
- How we turned chaos into culture
- How one idea, shared in a toolbox talk, changed the way a team worked

Those are the moments that matter. They inspire. They ripple out. So, if this book, or one of my talks, encourages just one person to say,

"Actually... I've got a story too," then that's success.

Because your story might be the one that sparks change in someone else. That's how the global reliability community grows and strengthens. That's how legacy is built.

THE REAL MEASURE OF A CAREER

After 40 years in maintenance and reliability, I've learned that actual progress isn't just measured in uptime or performance, it's found in the people you grow with, the lessons you pass on, and the quiet impact you leave behind.
Years from now, someone may still be using a method, mindset, or metric they learned from reading this book, attending one of our training courses, or listening to a conference talk.

That's the kind of impact that doesn't show up on a dashboard... but it lasts. That's legacy.

When you share your experience, you're not just passing on knowledge; you're connecting, inspiring, and helping to shape the future of reliability.
And that's how you know your career made a difference.

The Next Chapter is Yours

And so, my journey continues...

I'm still out there. Still learning, sharing, still teaching, still listening.

Maybe we'll meet at a conference, a training session, or somewhere along our shared journey...

Wherever we meet, just know this:

You're not alone in this journey. You're part of a global community of people who care deeply about doing things better. About keeping the world turning, one asset, one team, one insight at a time. Until then,

Keep your reliability passion high.
Keep your standards higher.
Fix the unfixable.
Solve the unsolvable.
Lubricate the unloved.
Plan with purpose
Protect the critical
And always...
Keep rocking with reliability.

– Gary Tyne CMRP

The Author

"Reliability isn't something you achieve once.
It's something you build every day."
– Gary Tyne

About the Author

Gary Tyne is the Founder and Director of Pro-Reliability Solutions, a UK and Ireland-based consultancy dedicated to helping organisations improve maintenance and reliability practices.

With over 40 years of global experience across industries like oil and gas, manufacturing, mining, and power generation, Gary is widely respected and recognised as an expert in maintenance and reliability engineering for his deep practical knowledge and grounded people-first approach.

He is known for his pragmatic approach to asset management, deep understanding of condition monitoring, and ability to connect with frontline teams and senior leadership.

He has worked on thousands of sites, trained countless professionals, and spoken at international conferences, always bringing real-world wisdom, sharp insights, and humour to the conversation.

It's this wealth of hard-earned experience that underpins his book, turning complex reliability challenges into relatable lessons and actionable insights.

So, if you're reading his book, you're getting decades of experience in the field distilled into lessons that aim to make life easier and assets more reliable for everyone in the maintenance world.

Gary's specialities include:

- Predictive and Preventive Maintenance
- Condition-Based Monitoring
- Asset Strategy Development (RCM, FMEA)
- Root Cause Analysis Facilitation
- Incident Investigation
- Building a Culture of Reliability
- Coaching Teams to Bridge the Gap Between Plans and Practice

His Philosophy:

Gary is known for no-nonsense, practical insights. He emphasises that real improvement doesn't come from theory alone; it comes from listening, learning, and doing the hard work, one step at a time.

His writing and training often blend real-world stories with lessons that stick, especially for teams working on the ground.

A THANK-YOU GIFT FOR READERS

With Gratitude for joining me on this journey , readers of this book can:

GIFT VOUCHER

Book a free 60-minute consultation with me, head to garytyne.com.

Click the Free Consultation button, and email me to lock in your slot.

GIFT VOUCHER

Enjoy 10% off selected training courses with Pro-Reliability Solutions Limited.

Claim your discount at pro-reliabilitysolutions.com

Simply book within 12 months of your purchase to claim your discount. This offer applies to course fees only, is non-transferable, and can't be combined with other discounts. Standard booking and cancellation policies apply.

REAL RESULTS, REAL MOMENTUM, NO FLUFF.

Testimonials

"The greatest achievements are rarely the work of one,
but the result of many
hearts and minds coming together."

I worked with Gary on a site-wide Reliability Project, which began with the building of a Reliability Block Diagram. We had a 60-day project plan, and with Gary's Reliability skills combined with Project Management, the initial phase was completed in 57 days. Gary then moved on to supporting the site's expansion project on the Cobalt recovery facility, which required a full 'Reliability in Design' approach during the design phase.

I wouldn't hesitate to recommend Gary and his practical, hands-on approach to reliability for any Manufacturing organisation, and wish him well with his future endeavours.

Andrew Lonsdale,
Reliability Specialist, Queensland, Australia

I first met Gary back in 2010; he was one of the people who interviewed me for a Reliability Engineer role at a large chemical manufacturing facility in Huddersfield. When I look back at this period, I classify it as "career-defining". Gary was instrumental in initiating my transformation from a Maintenance Engineer to a Reliability Engineer through his coaching, using his extensive knowledge of best-in-class reliability tools and his experience of how to employ them to drive results. Gary is, in my opinion, a true professional and innovative leader in the field of Maintenance and Reliability. Gary's coaching and advice still continue to this day. Whenever I need advice or a friendly chat, it is never too much trouble for Gary. His ethics are driven by wanting to do the right thing for the greater good.

Ian Price
Head of Operations and Maintenance, Qatar.

I worked with Gary for nearly three years. He is a highly motivated individual who is passionate about the proven reliability tools he uses to benefit his customers. He is excellent at transforming the mindset of Engineers into reliability-focused individuals.

A great person for creating the cultural change that is needed to get that "Competitive Advantage". The title of "Mr Reliability" is well deserved.

Gary Smith
Reliability Engineer – Owens Corning, UK

Having the opportunity to be part of the ITC ManEx project, I highly appreciate Gary's coaching and project leadership skills, as well as his valuable input to the Devnya Cement Reliability and Manufacturing Excellence journey. Excellent trainer, proved to be an expert in Reliability and Project management; the practical training sessions really helped. A great contributor to the implementation phases. Thanks, Gary, keep going!

Zhelyazko Kodzhabashev
Maintenance Manager, Bulgaria

In 2015, the Italcementi Group's Manufacturing Excellence Department launched a Global Plant Reliability Program. I was very pleased to have Gary supporting our team in developing and implementing the Program.

He delivered extremely valuable tools and training in Reliability Centred Maintenance. His contribution was a key factor in upgrading and enhancing the culture and skills of many Maintenance Managers and their teams. I appreciate his extensive experience in reliability and maintenance, as well as his strong leadership and communication skills.

Enrico Caputo
Organisational Development and Manufacturing Excellence Manager, Italy

I've known Gary as a colleague and friend for 14 years. A genuine bloke with a great sense of humour, Gary Tyne's new venture, Pro-Reliability Solutions, will always find the best way to improve the profitability of your business. He knows how to support businesses by working with key stakeholders and systematically addressing their concerns. He is a safety-minded practitioner with a wealth of expertise in reliability engineering and problem-solving. I have no hesitation in recommending Pro-Reliability Solutions to any business requiring a genuine, customer-focused service.

Peter McCoombe, Director
Safe Decisions Australia

It is with much enthusiasm that I recommend Gary for your asset reliability solutions.

Gary was the Project Manager on an International Project we collaborated on in France and the United States.

Gary's Reliability Engineering skills are truly phenomenal. He has excellent attention to detail and project leadership skills. Gary has a very special spark, and it was a great pleasure to be part of his team.

Steven M Stehr,
CMRP - Reliability Team Leader, Canada

Throughout my career, I have worked with various improvement tools and applications, including Kaizen, Fishbone, 6S, 5 Whys, and 3Cs. I have always felt that although these tools are good in their own right, they are not comprehensive enough to identify the actual Root Cause of a problem. In 2022, I was introduced to Pro Reliability Solutions, headed up by Gary Tyne. The primary reason for the meeting was to implement a method of Root Cause Analysis, more specifically, the Apollo Root Cause Analysis method developed by Dean L. Gano.

The initial approach was to perform a Root Cause Analysis on a problem. Gary, a colleague and I set up in a meeting room and started. From building a timeline, gathering data, collecting evidence, building a reality chart and developing an action plan to resolve some of the identified root causes, it is a transformational way to perform Root Cause Analysis.

It opens doors you might have overlooked, it allows you to question the primary concern, for example

- *We started at 'Product Quality Out of Spec', which moved to 'Unable to supply Customer', which moved to 'Liable to pay large fine to Customer', so when building the chart, rather than starting with the first, it would read like this.*
- *Liable to pay a fine to the customer, caused by the inability to supply the customer, caused by the Product quality being out of spec.*

From that point, the reality chart explodes into areas you never knew existed and covers a whole range of different areas that you may not have directly linked to the primary concern otherwise. It is a good tool, and used correctly, with the right triggers in place, can determine the difference between putting a plaster on something and truly discovering a Root Cause.

The application is easy to use, the methodology is consistent, and the outcome always delivers a number of actions and root causes. Once we had completed the initial RCA, several team members were selected to attend a three-day RCA workshop to learn how to perform RCA effectively.

We used examples from the workplace and generated some really good actions and identified some Root Causes that would have been left unidentified without RCA. Beyond this, we needed some facilitators who really took this method to heart. Two of my colleagues and I went on to attend the RCA master class for Facilitators. This class was great and builds confidence in leading RCA.

Having a facilitator keeps focus and ensures the team performing the RCA stays on track. Gary is a great coach and worked to enable us to perform RCA like never before in my workplace. If the Senior leadership team buy into RCA and the ARCA method, take the opportunity with both hands, it will change your work life when dealing with issues and concerns.

Thanks for everything, Gary. I look forward to working with you in the future.

Gareth Ellerby, Production Manager, AAK, UK

I have to say that when I sat in the room for my first introduction to the Apollo process, my mind was blown. I had the Gary quote, "light bulb moment". We didn't have an established RCA process in place, and we needed something to bring all area functions together to identify and agree on the root cause(s) and establish the necessary actions and solutions, which Apollo does. I was also very fortunate to complete the facilitator training with Pro-Reliability. This gives me a greater understanding of Apollo and extra skills in engaging and presenting.

Esther Moulson,
Technical Compliance Manager, AAK, UK

I first met Gary when I was working as a Maintenance Team Leader, and our company was still operating in a very reactive mode. He delivered a Root Cause Analysis course that left a lasting impression on me; not just because of the content, but because of the way he delivered it. Gary is a fantastic facilitator whose guidance comes directly from deep, hands-on experience. He's always precise, methodical, and convincing in his approach.

With a background in maintenance himself, Gary and I quickly found a common language. As I progressed in my own career in maintenance and reliability, Gary became a valuable mentor. He supported me with his knowledge, helped benchmark the current state of our factory, and worked with me to create a clear, achievable path toward reliability. His global experience with companies at all stages of the reliability journey meant that his advice was always relevant, practical, and grounded in reality.

Beyond his professional expertise, Gary is also a great person to be around, approachable, kind, and generous with his time and insight. He's always willing to offer thoughtful advice while respecting your own perspective and adapting to your approach. It's been a pleasure to learn from and work with him.

Maciej Janowski,
Head of Reliability, GA Pet Food Partners

I served my apprenticeship in a very reactive maintenance environment. While this approach honed my fault-finding skills, I never stopped to ask 'why'? Nor did we attempt to prevent future failures, and the reactive cycle continued.

When I met Gary from Pro-Reliability Solutions, he changed my entire perspective on maintenance, and I started a journey of reliability that I am still on to this day. PRS became my reliability partner, and working collaboratively, we have delivered many reliability projects together, shifting towards a proactive mindset, preventing failures, and reducing business risks. I hope to continue our collaboration for years to come.

Mark Maguire,
Engineering Manager, UK Food Company

I had the pleasure of working alongside Gary in Ireland many years ago, and his friendly, professional approach left a lasting impression. As the founder of Pro-Reliability Solutions in the UK, Gary is a true industry thought leader in reliability, root cause analysis, and asset management. His expertise and innovative insights continue to inspire excellence in the field.

Philip Sage,
Director, Mantua Group, Australia, Author of 'Maximo Managers Guide to Business Performance Management'

INDEX of Words

Index

Index

Index

Index

Index

Index

Index

Index

Index

The journey of reliability and maintenance doesn't end here, it begins anew with every challenge, every system, and every opportunity to improve.

If these lessons have sparked ideas, questions, or inspiration, I'd love to continue the conversation with you, because reliability is not just a practice, it's a mindset.

■ Email: info@pro-reliabilitysolutions.com
🌐 Website: garytyne.com
🌐 Company: pro-reliabilitysolutions.com
🔗 LinkedIn: linkedin.com/in/garytyne

Let's connect, collaborate,
&
keep the momentum alive.

Printed in Dunstable, United Kingdom

69112686R00218